Canadian
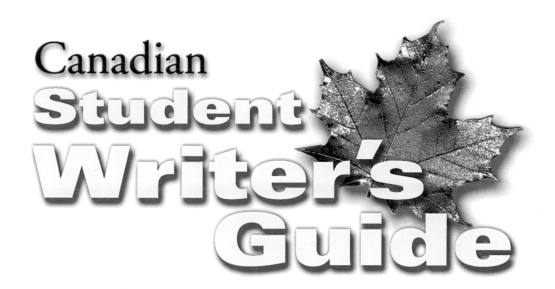

Chelsea Donaldson

gage EDUCATIONAL PUBLISHING COMPANY
A DIVISION OF CANADA PUBLISHING CORPORATION
Vancouver · Calgary · Toronto · London · Halifax

Canadian Cataloguing in Publication Data
Donaldson, Chelsea, 1959–
Gage Canadian student writer's guide

ISBN 0-7715-1318-6

1. English language – Composition and exercises – Juvenile literature.
2. English language – Grammar – Juvenile literature.   I. Title

PE1408.D615 1999   808′.042   C99-932456-X

Reviewers
The publisher gratefully acknowledges the contributions of the following educators to the *Gage Canadian Student Writer's Guide*:

Joan E. Alexander
St. Albert PSSD #6, AB

Patrick Lashmar
Hamilton–Wentworth RCDSB, ON

Steven E. Bland
Durham DSB #13, ON

Cam Macpherson
Toronto DSB, ON

Linda M. Coo
Calgary Board of Education, AB

Michael Ouellette
Annapolis Valley Regional SB, NS

June James
Surrey SD #36, BC

Harry Wagner
Parkland School Division #70, AB

Percy M. MacGougan, formerly Secondary Language Arts Consultant
PEI Dept. of Education

Publisher, Secondary Education: Janice Schoening
Editor: Evelyn Maksimovich
Cover and Text Design: Fizzz Design Inc.

We acknowledge the financial support of the Government of Canada through the Book Publishing Industry Development Program for our publishing activities.

ISBN 0-7715-**1318-6**
2 3 4 5 FP 03 02 01 00
Written, printed, and bound in Canada

Table of Contents

Writing Process

Contents

1

Purpose and Audience

Before you begin to write, make sure you have a clear idea of the purpose for your writing and the audience for whom you are writing. This will help you to determine the form of writing you should use. Some possible purposes for writing include the following:

to persuade	to describe	to amuse
to defend	to express	to entertain
to explain	to compare	to inform
to respond	to analyse	to educate
to question	to report	

Start by writing a sentence to remind you of your purpose, your audience, and your topic as you write. For example:

> I am writing…**to describe** *to my teacher and classmates* how I felt when our team won the soccer championship.

> I am writing…**to persuade** *readers of the Daily Herald* to donate emergency supplies to the disaster relief fund.

The audience you are writing for will also influence what you write and how you write it. If, for example, you think your readers will agree with you on a certain issue, the words you choose, the tone you adopt, and the order in which you present your ideas will probably be different from a piece written for people who you think will disagree with you.

Choosing a Topic

There are many ways to find a topic for your writing. Try

• reading books or magazines

• browsing the Internet or scanning an encyclopedia

- watching videos or television shows
- flipping through your journal
- rereading your class notes
- brainstorming with a group of four or five classmates
- talking with a friend or family member
- drawing an idea web using general key words

Once you have found a possible topic, use the following questions to check that it is appropriate:

- Is it a topic you find interesting?
- Do you know (or can you find) enough information about the topic?
- Can you narrow down the topic enough so that you can write about it in the space and time you have available?
- Does the topic meet any special requirements set by your teacher?

Writing a Thesis Sentence

A thesis sentence tells what you want to say about the topic you have chosen. It doesn't just *state* the topic, it says something *about* it. A well-worded thesis sentence can give your readers some useful clues about what they are about to read. It can also suggest the form of writing you have chosen (e.g., narration, description, exposition, persuasion) and indicate how the piece is organized (e.g., in stages, by examples, etc.). Most thesis sentences appear in the first or second paragraph.

Topic: Hockey Violence

Thesis for a Persuasive Essay	Thesis for a Report	Thesis for an Instructional Manual
Injuries and fights are unavoidable in a rough game such as hockey. OR There is no reason why anyone should be injured playing hockey.	According to statistics, hockey violence is not as widespread as everyone believes.	To avoid injury in hockey, you need to keep your head up, your eyes moving, and your mind alert.

Organizing Information

How you arrange your information or ideas depends on what you are writing (the form), why you are writing (the purpose), and for whom you are writing (the audience). Here are some common patterns of organization:

Patterns of Organization	Examples
time sequence (chronological)	stories factual accounts
place or location (spatial)	descriptions of people, places, or things
features or characteristics	comparisons descriptions of people, places, or things
order of importance	news stories business reports memos persuasive writing
cause to effect or vice versa	science reports explanations or instructions

Outlining

An outline is like a map to help guide you through your writing. Several ways of creating an outline for your writing follow. Use the text outline or tree diagram for most non-fiction writing, such as reports and essays; use a time line for narratives, such as short stories or biographies.

Text Outline

I. Main Idea

   A. Supporting Idea

       1. Detail or example

           a) specific information

           b) specific information

       2. Detail or example

           a) specific information

           b) specific information

   B. Supporting Idea

       1. Detail or example

             …etc.

Tree Diagram

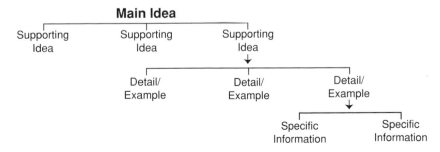

Time Line

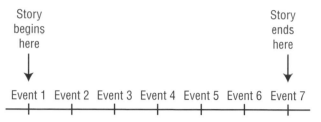

Taking Notes

If you need to gather information from books or other sources
before you write, follow these guidelines for taking notes:
See Research, p. 56.

- **Focus on your purpose.** It is easy to become interested in areas
  that are not relevant to your needs. Remind yourself often of your
  purpose for writing.

- **Look for the structure.** Look for clues that show how the
  information is organized. Headings and key phrases such as "There
  are three main reasons why…" or "The main stages in the process
  are…" signal that the reasons or stages will be explained in the
  paragraphs that follow.

- **Make connections.** Try writing your notes in outline form to show
  how the ideas are related. You might also use a web to record
  main ideas and supporting details, or other graphic organizers, such
  as a Venn diagram or mind map. If you're taking notes directly into
  a computer, you can group related information by using simple
  formatting, such as boldface or italic headings, or bulleted or
  numbered lists.

- **Write in your own words.** Avoid repeating word-for-word what
  you have read. If you want to use a direct quote from a source, put
  it in quotation marks and note the source (title, page number).

- **Identify the source.** Write the name of the author, the title of the source, and the date of publication. For a book, also include where it was published and the name of the publisher. This information can be found on the copyright page near the beginning of the book. If you are using only one section of a longer work, write down the page numbers as well.

  Remember, no matter what you are using—a book, a magazine, the Internet, or a CD-ROM—it's much easier to record the source information as you go than it is to try to retrieve it later on. **See Citations and Footnotes, p. 64.**

- **Use few words.** Skip small words such as *the* altogether, and develop your own shorthand to save you time. For example:

Try this...	As shorthand for...
=	is
<	less than / small
>	more than / big
Ø	nothing / none / no
b/c	because
nr.	near
s/b	should be
w/o	without

- **Use cue cards.** If you're taking notes from several sources, try recording each fact on a separate card. By sorting and re-arranging groups of cards, you can experiment with different ways of organizing the information. (You can follow this same method if you are taking notes on a computer by cutting and pasting until you find an arrangement that works.)

Write a shortened form or abbreviation of the source on the top of each card and record the full source information on a separate sheet. What follows is a sample note card showing one fact taken from this source: *Alexander Graham Bell: An Inventive Life* by Elizabeth MacLeod.

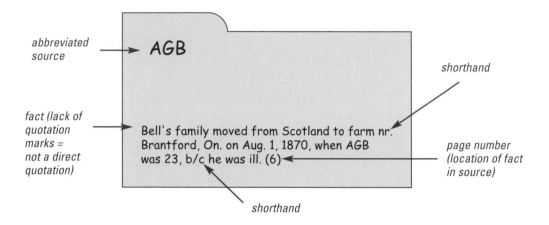

abbreviated source → **AGB**

shorthand

fact (lack of quotation marks = not a direct quotation) → Bell's family moved from Scotland to farm nr. Brantford, On. on Aug. 1, 1870, when AGB was 23, b/c he was ill. (6)◄

page number (location of fact in source)

shorthand

Writing an Effective Beginning

The first paragraph of an essay or research report tells your readers what you are writing about, and what you want to say about it. It should also catch your audience's interest and make them want to read on. Here are some suggestions for creating interest in your topic:

- Present a scene that illustrates the topic or raises a question related to it ("Imagine waking up one morning to feel the floor shaking and see your books falling off your shelves").

- Present an interesting or amazing fact that leads into your thesis.

- Relate the topic to the lives of your readers ("We usually think of earthquakes as happening elsewhere, to other people, but according to experts, one could happen here at any time").

- Tell a joke or funny story that is related to your topic—unless humour is out of place because your topic is serious or tragic.

- Promise to reveal something later on in the essay ("Later, I'll discuss what you can do to prepare for an earthquake").

For a narrative, you might try creating interest in one of the following ways:

- Begin at an interesting or suspenseful moment in the middle of the story and fill in the details later.

> When Grandmama died at eighty-three our whole household held its breath. She had promised us a sign of her leaving, final proof that her present life had ended well. My parents knew that without any clear sign, our own family fortunes could be altered, threatened.
> My stepmother looked endlessly into the small cluttered room the ancient lady had occupied. Nothing was touched, nothing changed.
> My father, thinking that a sign should appear in Grandmama's garden, looked at the frost-killed shoots and cringed: *no, that could not be it.…*
>
> from "The Jade Peony" by Wayson Choy

- Begin with some dialogue that establishes characters, introduces conflict, and/or provides background information. In the following example, we get an immediate impression of the three girls and of Cindy, based on a few lines of dialogue.

> "Cin, Cin, Cindy!" the three girls call out.
>
> "Cindy! Will you help me put up the decorations for the dance?" Agnes says.
>
> "Could you find my scissors, Cindy?" Marybeth chimes in.
>
> "We need more cups!" Dara cries. "Cindy, where are the cups?"
>
> Cindy hurries over. "Here I come, Agnes," she says in a low voice. "Okay, Marybeth. I'll find them, Dara."…
>
> from "The Transformations of Cindy R." by Anne Mazer

- Begin with a startling image or description.

> The flying saucer landed on Fred Foster's back lawn at three o'clock on a Saturday afternoon. Fred's oldest daughter, Mona, answered the door. There was a little green man standing there; he had a bald head, bulbous eyes, huge ears, and a pair of antennae protruding from his forehead. He was wearing a goldfish bowl on his head. She recognized him at once as a Martian....
>
> from "The Day the Martian Landed" by Pierre Berton

If you are having difficulty writing the beginning of a piece, try writing it *after* you have written everything else. Many writers find that writing the beginning last is easier because they know exactly what they have said and can see how it all fits together.

Drafting Tips

Once you have chosen a topic and gathered information, you need to write a first draft. This may seem overwhelming—lots of writers will tell you that *starting* to write is the biggest hurdle they have to overcome. Here are some suggestions to help jump-start your writing:

- Don't worry too much about the quality of your writing—yet. Although it's important, it's not the main focus at this stage. For now, just concentrate on getting your ideas down on paper.

- Start wherever you feel most comfortable. If you find it difficult to write the first paragraph, begin with another section and fill in the blanks later.

- If you get stuck and don't know what to write next, try recopying what you have written (print it out if you're working on a computer). You might also try explaining to a friend what you want to say, or move on to another section or paragraph.

- Just before you start to write, read something. If you choose a piece of writing in the same genre that is well written, and that has the tone you want to create in your own work, you'll probably find yourself imitating that style. For example, if you are writing a newspaper article, try reading the front section of a well-respected newspaper before you begin.

- Try to follow your outline as much as possible, but make changes to it if necessary. You may find, for example, that you have so much information to include in a section that you need to expand that section into two parts; or, you might discover as you write that a different order works better.

Revising Tips

Revising your first draft means looking at the big picture, then adding, deleting, and re-arranging as necessary. If possible, set aside your draft for a day or two before you begin revising it. Doing so will allow you to see your work with fresh eyes.

Here are some guidelines to follow when you come to the revision stage:

- Check that everything you have written relates to your purpose.

- Make sure you have included enough background information for your audience.

- Re-arrange paragraphs and sentences to create a logical flow.

- Cut or add information to get your message across in the best way possible.

- Add connecting words to make the relationships among your ideas clear.

- Make small stylistic changes (for example, changing words or phrases, adding and deleting sentences, correcting mistakes) as you notice them, but don't spend too much time looking for these. They will be your focus in the editing stage, the next step in the writing process.

- If possible, get feedback on your work from other readers. Consider their comments and suggestions, and decide what changes you need to make.

Editing Tips

The revising and editing stages of the writing process may overlap, but they are not the same. Generally, revising deals with focus, content, and organization, while editing looks in more detail at words, sentences, and the flow of the writing.

When you edit, follow these guidelines:

- Look for ways to say what you want using as few words as possible.

- Fine-tune your choice of words to suit your purpose and your audience. Pay attention not only to what the words *mean*, but what they *connote*. **See Connotation and Denotation, p. 79.**

- Check that you have used a consistent voice (first person, third person), tense (present or past), and style (level of formality, reading level, flow, and so on).

- Correct any mistakes in grammar, mechanics, or spelling as you notice them. Avoid spending too much time looking for these errors, however; there will be plenty of time for that at the proofreading stage of the process.

Proofreading Tips

Proofreading is the final stage in the writing process. It involves preparing your work to be published. Editing and proofreading tend to overlap, just as revising and editing do; nevertheless, set aside some time at the end of the process to focus on proofreading alone.

When you proofread, try to do the following:

- Read slowly, focussing on each word. (If you used a computer to prepare your written piece, proofread a hard copy rather than reading your work on screen.)

- Check for errors in capitalization, punctuation, and spelling. Double-check items that have been troublesome in the past.

- Check that all place names and proper names are spelled correctly.

- Make sure you have used quotation marks correctly.

- Spend extra time checking lists, charts, and tables to make sure the content is accurate and set up properly.

- Check that each paragraph is indented, and that each sentence begins with a capital letter.

- Acknowledge all your sources correctly and completely.

- Recopy or print your work in a suitable format (for example, using correct letter style for a business letter, adding a title page for an essay or report, and so on).

- Ask a classmate to proofread your work again to make sure you haven't missed anything.

Proofreading Symbols

Use the symbols that follow to mark changes to your writing.

∧	insert	The house ˢis on fire.
ℯ	delete	Rattlesnakes are very verry dangerous.
∼	transpose (switch)	Raisa, Louise, and Karin are 12, 14, and 16 years old, respectively.
≡	capital	Planet earth may be in danger.
/	lower case	We Compost all our food scraps.
¶	new paragraph	So that day ended badly. The next day...
⊙	add period	Liu wondered which way to go ⊙
⋏	add comma	Bring your tent a sleeping bag, and a flashlight.
⋎	add apostrophe	"Its Hans!" he cried.
#	add space	Danieland I are leaving tomorrow.
⌒	close space	Chickens can't fly, but duc ks can.
....	stet (don't delete)	The pictures are not ready.

Organizing Your Time

Learn to manage your time and you'll be well on your way to getting better marks. Here are some ways that will help you to keep track of your assignments and use your time more efficiently.

- Use a journal or an agenda to keep track of due dates. Get in the habit of looking at your agenda every day.

- Use the amount of time you are given to complete an assignment as a clue to what your teacher expects. If you are assigned a writing project today that is due tomorrow, chances are you will not be expected to do a lot of research or to write a lengthy piece. You will, however, be expected to present ideas that are well thought through, well written, and carefully proofread. On the other hand, if you have a month to complete the assignment, budget more time for research or preparation, be prepared to develop your ideas in more detail, and spend more time revising your writing. Whatever the assignment, make sure you understand exactly what is expected, and by when.

- Break down big assignments into smaller tasks, and estimate the amount of time you will need for each stage. For example, if you are writing a research paper, you will probably need to set aside about half the time you have available for prewriting (that is, preparing to write a draft), including the actual research. The other half can be divided among drafting, revising, editing, and proofreading.

- Set aside a particular time and place for homework assignments and stick to your schedule. Not only will a regular routine help you to concentrate when it is time to work, it will also help you to relax when it isn't.

- Remember that "the perfect is the enemy of the good." Although it is important to challenge yourself, it is equally important to have reasonable goals so that you can achieve what you set out to do.

Forms

Contents

2

Narrative Writing

Narrative writing tells what happened. Some types of narratives are novels, short stories, records of events, ballads, folk tales, myths, legends, biographies, autobiographies, and plays.

Purpose

The purpose of narration is to tell a story.

Organization

- Narratives usually have a beginning, in which the characters, setting, and conflict are introduced; a middle, in which the conflict intensifies; and an end, in which the conflict is resolved.

- Details are usually arranged in chronological (time) order. Storywriters often begin at an exciting point somewhere in the middle of the action, and use **flashbacks**—scenes from an earlier time that are either remembered by a character, or simply related by the narrator—to fill in information about what has already happened.

Style

- Most narratives are written in the first or third person. Choose the point of view for your narrative carefully. Remember that a first-person (*I*) narrator can move the reader to sympathize with the character who is telling the story, but can also give a limited—and not always reliable—view of what is happening. Third-person (*she, he, they, it*) narrators can be more objective and may have a broader view of the action, but they may also be less sympathetic to the characters' feelings.

- One way to heighten the suspense and create a sense of unity in a story is to use **foreshadowing**: words, images, or events that give clues about what is going to happen. For example, if something bad is about to happen to your characters, you might describe a cloud suddenly blocking out the sun, or a sinister movement in the shadows.

- Try to tell your story, at least in part, through dialogue (the words of the characters). Dialogue adds interest and variety to narrative writing.

- The pace of a narrative—how fast or slow the action moves along—is crucial to getting and holding the reader's attention. If the plot moves too slowly, readers will lose interest.

The following anecdote relates a simple comic incident. The writer has included enough detail ("backed away and swallowed hard") to make the scene vivid and realistic, and to emphasize the astonishment of the main character. However, unnecessary information—anything that might make the punch line at the end lose its humour—has been omitted. Notice how the story is told, in part, through dialogue.

Sample Narrative Piece

McWilliams was driving along a narrow country road when his engine simply stopped running. He got out of the car and opened the hood. Since he was anything but an expert on cars, he stared at the engine for several seconds. Suddenly, he heard a voice behind him.

"It's the fuel-injection system," the voice said.

McWilliams turned and saw no one. The only sign of life was a cow standing on the other side of a fence. McWilliams looked around. Then the cow repeated, "It's the fuel-injection system."

McWilliams stared, his eyes widening and his mouth dropping open. "Why are you standing there looking like a fool?" the cow said. "Check the fuel injectors."

McWilliams backed away and swallowed hard. Then he ran up a path that led to a farmhouse at the top of a hill. He pounded on the door until a man opened it.

"Calm down, mister," the man said. "What seems to be the trouble?"

"My car..." McWilliams stammered. "My car broke down. I got out to look at the car..."

"Yes?" the man said impatiently.

"Your cow!" McWilliams sputtered. "Your cow said to me, 'It's the fuel-injection system'!"

"Ignore it," the man said calmly. "That animal doesn't know a thing about cars."

from *The Random House Book of Jokes and Anecdotes: For Speakers, Managers, and Anyone Who Needs a Laugh*, edited by Joseph Claro

Descriptive Writing

Description is often included in longer pieces of writing, such as narratives. Examples of descriptive writing include character sketches, setting or place descriptions, and travelogues. Many poems are also descriptive.

Purpose

Generally, the purpose of descriptive writing is to create a single overall image or impression of a person, a place, a thing, or an idea.

Organization

- One way to organize a description is spatially. For example, you might describe a room by imagining what you would see if you were standing in the doorway, looking from the left-hand side to the right. More often, however, you would begin with some obvious, striking, or important feature (for instance, an impressive fireplace directly opposite the door of the room) and then describe what surrounds it. This arrangement is still spatial; it just begins from a different place.

- Descriptive details can also be arranged in order of importance, or prominence. If, for example, you are describing someone's face, you might begin with a general comment and then select features that back up your assessment, as the author of the sample descriptive piece (facing page) has done. Note that the features the author selected are not in any clear spatial order; instead, she focusses on details here and there, almost as they would strike you if you were looking at the subject yourself.

Style

- The words and images in a description should appeal to as many of your readers' senses as possible: sight, hearing, touch, taste, and smell.

- Similes, metaphors, and other forms of figurative language can help to evoke clear images in the minds of your readers.

- Descriptive writers choose details that help to create the overall impression they want the reader to experience. Don't leave out important details in your description, but do try to relate them to the theme or impression you are trying to create.

Notice how the author of the following description lets the physical details of the mother's face tell us something about her character. Details such as the "firm chin line" and the fact that she looks "as though she were loosely clenching her teeth" give the impression that she is strong-willed, and has perhaps had a hard life, without the narrator actually telling us so. On the other hand, her full lips and the fact that she "did not exactly frown," coupled with her compassion toward her children, imply that, although she may not be happy, she has a generous heart.

Sample Descriptive Piece

…Ma was a tall, rangy woman. She had a strong handsome face, with high cheekbones and a good firm chin line. Her lips were full. Her teeth were her own, although she smiled so rarely that you seldom saw them; her mouth tended to be held in a set straight line. She did not exactly frown; it was more as though she were loosely clenching her teeth. Her eyes were veiled, as if she had shut herself off from her surroundings and was thinking either private thoughts or nothing at all. Oh, she was kind enough and gentle enough when we needed it, though perhaps we needed it more often than she knew. But when we had cut knees or tonsillectomies, or when friends broke our hearts, she would hold us and hug us. Her mouth would lose its hard tight shape, and her eyes would come alive with concern and love.

Her lovely crisp auburn hair was short and unshaped making her face look uncompromising and austere. She wore baggy slacks over her excellent legs, and she owned two shabby grey sweaters and two faded graceless blouses. I did not ask myself why my mother looked this way, or why she had retreated behind her frozen face. One accepts one's parents for a long time, without theory or question. Speculation comes later, with adolescence and all the uncertainty and confusion it brings.…

from "The Leaving" by Budge Wilson

Expository Writing

Expository writing is writing that gives the reader information. You use exposition when you write instructions, lab reports, explanations, news stories, or research reports.

Purpose

The general purpose of expository writing is to present information. The more specific reason for writing an expository piece may be to explain, to instruct, to report, to analyse, to compare, to define, to evaluate, or to inform.

Organization

- Expository pieces use logical patterns of organization. News reports present the most important information first; instructions are arranged step-by-step; scientific explanations usually move from cause to effect, or vice versa.

- When you are deciding how to organize your expository writing, ask yourself what arrangement would be most useful to your reader. Consider including a summary or overview of the most important information at the beginning of the piece, then fill in the details in later sections. Use headings to help make the information easier to find.

Style

- Expository writing focusses on facts, not your own opinions. However, the opinions of other people—especially experts or authorities—are acceptable. (If the experts disagree, be sure to include all sides of the argument.)

- Expository pieces are usually written in the third person (*she, he, they, it*). Instructions, however, use the second person (*you*).

- The **tone** of an expository piece is usually objective. Avoid words that have strong connotations—either positive or negative.

- The language you use in expository writing should be geared to the level of understanding of the audience. If your intended readers are familiar with your topic, then you are free to use technical terms as necessary. In writing aimed at a more general audience, however, either explain technical terms or avoid them altogether.

Notice how the writer of the following excerpt from a magazine article explains the concept of saturation diving and describes the technical process of decompression by comparing them with something familiar to his readers (a sponge and a balloon losing air, respectively).

Sample Expository Piece

The concept of saturation diving explains how aquanauts can live inside *Aquarius* for extended time periods. Your body tissues, muscle and fat, are like a sponge. No matter how long a sponge stays in a bucket of water, it only absorbs a certain amount of liquid. The same goes for your body tissues. Saturation divers only absorb a certain amount of nitrogen and other inert, or slow dissolving, gases in their tissues no matter how long they stay submerged at a certain depth. That's why aquanauts only need to decompress at the end of their mission.

Aquanauts are required to undergo a seventeen-hour decompression period after completing a ten-day mission in *Aquarius*. While the actual lab never leaves the bottom, the air pressure inside *Aquarius* is gradually adjusted until the lab's pressure is the same as air pressure at the surface. This allows the inert gas bubbles to dissolve out of body tissues without causing any problems. Think of it like this: if you have a balloon with a small leak in it, and you step on it, softly at first and then gradually harder, the air will seep out at a nice even pace. If you stomp on the balloon, however, you'll probably cause some serious physical damage.

from "Undersea Science" by Thomas Potts

Persuasive Writing

Persuasive writing tries to convince the reader to do or believe something. We are surrounded by persuasive messages in the form of advertisements; you may have written persuasive essays, speeches, book or movie reviews, editorials, or letters to the editor.

Purpose

The purpose of persuasion is to convince the reader to believe something or to take some action.

Organization

- Persuasive writing is usually arranged to emphasize the most important or strongest arguments in favour of the thesis.

- If your audience is likely to disagree with what you have to say, and you think you need to win them over, try beginning and ending with your strongest arguments. Put weaker arguments in the middle.

- If your readers are likely to agree with you, build enthusiasm by moving from your weakest points to your strongest.

Style

- Writers of persuasive pieces don't try to include every possible argument in their writing; instead, they choose the ones that they feel will be most convincing to their intended readers.

- The tone you choose in a persuasive piece helps to establish how trustworthy and believable you are. If readers dislike your attitude, they will be less likely to accept your arguments. The tone of a persuasive piece can be humorous, rational, angry, serious, insistent, indignant, sarcastic, enthusiastic—it all depends on how you wish to come across.

- While strong arguments backed up by facts or logic are essential, appeals to emotion are also important, especially if you want to rouse your readers to action.

- You can appeal to emotion by using **loaded words**—words that have strong good or bad associations (connotations).

- Emotional appeals can also be created by citing universal needs, wants, and values ("We all agree that war is a terrible thing…"), or by including personal experiences, made-up scenarios, or specific examples. The model that follows begins by appealing to our need for a winter holiday. It later uses specific examples of what might happen on Rest Day to make the idea seem more appealing (and humorous!) to the reader.

Sample Persuasive Piece

Canadians often complain about the lack of a long weekend between New Year's Day and Easter. It is paradoxical that the longest period of the year without a break is also the most difficult one in terms of climate. In any case, Canada has fewer public holidays than the U.S. and most countries in Europe.

Therefore, it is high time that Canada created a new holiday for the dead of winter, beyond half-baked innovations such as Flag Day and Heritage Day that have not caught on.

We suggest that the last Monday of February be declared "Rest Day," a day dedicated to sleep, relaxation, even laziness. On Rest Day, Canadians would be required to sleep in late, spend an inordinate part of their day in their pajamas, and have a late breakfast or brunch.

In the afternoon, many might enjoy a nap, and perhaps an early bed-time that evening. Rest Day Eve sleepovers would become *de rigueur*, at least for children old enough not to wake up their parents in the morning. Grown-ups could be invited to attend such activities, though many would elect to organize more formal brunches.…

Another advantage of Rest Day is that it would cross religious, ethnic, linguistic, regional, and class boundaries in honouring something common to all Canadians: the need to rest.…

Our politicians should establish Rest Day as the mid-winter break that Canadians need. We don't need religious, civil, or historical justification for taking a day off in February. Rather, the holiday should be honest and direct about its aim: keep Canadians in bed longer that morning.

from "Let's hear it (softly) for Rest Day" by Josie Marino and Jean-Francois Rioux

Short Story

A short story is a fictional tale that involves some form of conflict and resolution. Short stories can be as short as half a page, although most are longer than that. Virtually every kind of story that can be told in a novel can also be told in a short story. However, because of the length restrictions they face, writers of short stories must make every sentence count.

Purpose and Audience

The main purposes of a short story are to entertain the reader and express the writer's view of life through fiction. The age and interests of the intended readers affect the detail, theme, plot, level of language, and point of view of the story.

Organization

- Short stories are organized according to time sequence. The story may begin at any point in the sequence of events. Events that happened before the story begins are explained as the story unfolds.

- Sometimes authors use flashbacks to introduce an event that happened at an earlier time. At other times, the reader learns what happened from what the characters say to one another, or from explanations provided by the narrator, or both.

Style

When you write or read a short story, pay attention to how the following elements relate to one another.

- **Plot:** This is what happens in the story. Is it believable? Does the action move quickly enough? Does it come to a satisfying and logical conclusion?

- **Character:** Characters are revealed mainly through what they say and do, what others say about them, and how others react to them. Other elements can also contribute to creating a believable character: physical appearance, setting (for example, an urban apartment building versus a log cabin in the mountains), belongings, habits or characteristics, and ways of talking. In the excerpt on page 30, notice how the author establishes the personality of Jon right away, by reporting what he is doing (and not doing) and how he is feeling.

- **Setting:** The setting—where the story takes place—is the backdrop for the plot, but it can also contribute to the theme, the mood, and even the characters in a story. A story set in a graveyard at midnight, for example, already raises our expectations regarding what might happen, and sets a definite mood.

- **Conflict:** The conflict in a short story arises out of the characters and the situation. The main character may be in conflict with another character; with him- or herself; or with some outside force, such as nature (for example, a character may be struggling to survive during a flood or other disaster).

- **Theme:** The theme of a story is the overall message about human nature or life that the author wants to convey. It is expressed through all the elements of the story: the plot, the characters, the setting, and the conflict.

- **Mood:** The mood of a story is the feeling or attitude that it expresses (for example, sad, cheerful, dark, thoughtful, menacing). Writers establish mood through the words they choose, their descriptions of characters, and through the setting of the story.

- **Point of View:** Short story writers can write from many different points of view. The narrator of a short story may be a character in the story itself, writing the narrative in the first person (*I, me*). Other stories are written from the point of view of one of the characters, but using the third person (*he, she, they, it*). Still other stories have a third-person narrator who knows everything, and who can tell the reader what any character is thinking or doing at any time. This omniscient (all-seeing) type of narrator can report what is happening in two different places at the same time, and can compare the thoughts of different characters to the same events, as in the excerpt from a science fiction short story that follows. In the first paragraph, we see a scene from Jon's point of view; in the next, the narrator describes the same scene from the point of view of his sister, Peri.

> The heliolites soared above the river valley, clustering, separating. To Jon, squinting up into the sunshine, they were like a cloud of brilliant butterflies. For just a moment he wished he were up there with them, but only for a moment. The one time he'd soared he'd felt so nauseated that he'd barely made it back to solid earth in one piece. The nausea, along with a hatred of crowds, seemed to be the flip side of his "gift." He'd gladly trade the shameful hidden skill of telekinesis for the chance to soar with his sister and his best friend. To be skilled in telepathy and telekinesis, gifts useful only to spies and other servants of the state, was a burden he would happily cast off. To be like Peri. To be free...
>
> Peri, strapped in her harness, watched the city swing beneath her, a slowly rotating jigsaw of ceramic roofs, solar panels, and streets, with the river cutting a random furrow through its geometric order. Directly below her she could see Jon, a dark dot on the field by the bridge. Kid brother, isolated as usual from the crowd....
>
> from "And the Lucky Winner Is..." by Monica Hughes

Script

A script is the written text of a play, movie, television show, or other dramatic presentation. It contains dialogue (spoken words) as well as directions that tell what actions, sounds, images, or events should take place on the stage or screen as the words are being spoken.

Purpose and Audience

The purpose of a script is to tell a story through dialogue (the characters' spoken words) and action. The audience consists of those who will watch the script being performed.

Organization

- Dramatic scripts, like short stories, are organized around a conflict that involves one or more of the characters.

- The beginning introduces the characters and the setting, and sets up the situation or conflict.

- The middle of the script tells what happens when the conflict gets worse (this is called the *climax*).

- The end shows how the conflict is resolved (the *anticlimax*).

- Scripts are divided into scenes. Just as every paragraph in an essay or report has to relate back to the main idea, so every scene in a play must have a purpose: to develop a character, set the mood, or move the plot along. Begin a new scene whenever the setting, the time, or the point of view changes.

Style

Scripts share all the main features of short stories in that they require conflict, characters, setting, plot, and theme to work together. However, where a short story relies heavily on the narrator to provide information about the thoughts and feelings of the characters, scriptwriters have to rely largely on dialogue and action. To help compensate for these limitations, scripts—especially plays—use certain conventions that are not found in other forms of fiction.

- A **monologue** (a long, uninterrupted speech by one actor) can be used as a way of focussing the audience's attention on one character's thoughts or experiences. It is also a good way to introduce background information about the character or plot. However, too many monologues will slow down the pace of your script and make it sound artificial.

- **Soliloquies** (speeches made by one character to him- or herself or directly to the audience) can be used to reveal a character's inner thoughts or motives. Hamlet's famous speech that begins "To be or not to be; that is the question" is a soliloquy.

- In some plays, a **narrator or chorus** (group of narrators) stands outside the action and occasionally offers background information, commentary, or other explanations that might be handled by the narrator in a novel or short story. Remember, though, that using a narrator will distance your audience from the action and remind them that they are watching a play.

- **Stage directions** are used to set the scene, suggest what a character is doing while he or she is talking, or indicate sounds or events. Sometimes playwrights include stage directions within a passage of dialogue to give the actor directions.

Format

- Begin with a list of the characters in the play. You may want to include a brief description of the more important characters.

- Each time you change to a new location, describe the new setting briefly at the beginning of the scene.

- Identify who is speaking by writing that character's name in capital letters on the left-hand side of the page. (Keep in mind that scripts do not require the use of quotation marks to show that a character is speaking.) Often, playwrights will also use capitals for a character's name mentioned in stage directions.

- Use underlining for stage directions if you are handwriting the script; otherwise, use italics. Set off stage directions from the dialogue by putting them in parentheses.

- Use a long dash (—) or ellipsis points (…) to show that a speech is interrupted or unfinished.

Biography and Autobiography

A biography is writing about someone's life. A biography about the writer's own life is called an *autobiography*. Biographies and autobiographies present real events from the life of the subject. The events the writer chooses to include usually provide some insight into the thoughts, feelings, development, or importance of the person being described, or the times in which he or she lived.

Purpose and Audience

The purpose of most biographies and autobiographies is, first of all, to entertain. For example, when movie stars and other celebrities write their autobiographies, they know that their readers will want to know all about their meetings with other famous people, and what they themselves are like in private life.

Biographers, however, also select incidents that they feel give insight into their subject's personality. For example, a biographer who wants to give the impression that a political leader is untrustworthy might describe an incident from the leader's childhood in which he or she was caught cheating on a test. Someone with a more positive view of the leader might dismiss the incident as unimportant, or omit it altogether.

Organization

- Biographies and autobiographies are arranged chronologically (in time order). The writer selects the events he or she thinks are most relevant.

- When you write a biography or autobiography, try to give a sense of how much time has passed between incidents. For example, if you say "After we moved from the Philippines, we lived in England for a while and then moved to Canada," your reader has no sense of how much time you spent in England. It could be years, months, or days.

Style

When you write the story of your own or somebody else's life, remember the following:

- Focus on the facts, but include as much detail as you can to make it interesting. It is the details that will make your reader want to know more. If you are writing a biography, try to pick up interesting or revealing details by interviewing the subject (the person about whom you are writing) or someone close to him or her.

- Decide how you want to present your subject, then choose words and situations that will help to create the impression you want your readers to have of your subject.

- Avoid telling your reader what an incident means or says about the person. Instead, let the person's actions and words speak for themselves.

- Use brief quotations (from interviews, books, or magazine articles, for example) to create interest.

> I can only imagine what the people in the park thought when they saw my grandfather flying along the pathway in that rickety, hand-built machine. I suspect at least some of them must have had the fright of their lives! My father, who was twelve at the time, was horrified: "I figured I would never be able to show my face in town again," he explained.

- Always be sure to identify who made the comment, and to use his or her words without changing their meaning. If someone once said that your subject had "an extraordinary ability to get into trouble," don't quote that person as saying your subject had "extraordinary ability."

Poem

Poetry takes many forms: from highly structured sonnets, to free verse; from simple two-line couplets to hundred-page epics. What all poetic forms have in common is the way in which the language is used—it is often more vivid and intense than in prose or everyday speech. Poets achieve this goal in all sorts of ways: through figures of speech, rhythm (metre), rhyme, word sounds, allusions, even punctuation and the way the poem is set on the page.

Purpose and Audience

The purpose of a poem varies widely; it may be to tell a story, express an emotion, describe a scene, or simply to play with words. Most poems are intended to evoke some kind of emotional reaction in the audience, and all poems aim to achieve their purpose in the most intense, compact, and efficient way possible. While it is possible to write a poem for no one but yourself, most poems are meant to be read aloud to an audience.

Organization

- Poems are sometimes arranged in verses. Verses may consist of an equal number of lines, or they may vary in length. Consider starting a new verse when the rhyming pattern repeats itself, or leave a line break to show that the topic or point of view is changing, just as you would begin a new paragraph of an essay.

- Poems don't usually follow the rules of punctuation that apply to prose works. Because most poems are meant to be read aloud, poets may use line breaks and punctuation to show where the reader should pause, or to create rhythm. Breaking lines in order to form shapes on the page is another way that poets play with the rules.

Style

Here are some stylistic concerns to think about when you write a poem:

- **Rhyme:** Some poems rhyme; others don't. Poems that rhyme usually have a regular rhyming pattern, such as *abab*, in which the first and third lines rhyme, and the second and fourth lines rhyme.

I never saw a purple **cow**	*a*
I never hope to *see one*	*b*
But I can tell you any**how**	*a*
I'd rather see than *be one*.	*b*

- **Metre:** Metre is the rhythm of a poem when it is read aloud. Poets create metre through the pattern of stressed (-) and unstressed (-) syllables they choose. Notice the metre in the following excerpt from William Blake's "The Tyger."

> Tyger! Tyger! Burning bright
>
> In the forests of the night,
>
> What immortal hand or eye
>
> Could frame thy fearful symmetry?

In contrast, some poems simply imitate the rhythm of everyday speech:

The Big Saw
by Milton Acorn

Many's the time when I was on the job
The sawman came to me:
"You're able—And you can work fast.
Why don't you handle the big saw?"

Upon which I'd hold up my hands
Thumbs and fingers spread out:
"Look. Count 'em. Ten isn't there?
That's how many there's going to be!"

- **Imagery:** To say what they want to say using as few words as possible, poets often use figurative language, such as similes and metaphors.

- **Diction:** Poets choose their words carefully, taking into account the connotations as well as the way the words sound. **See Connotation and Denotation, p. 79.**

- **Sensory details:** Poets often try to get the reader to feel something. One way to evoke strong feelings is to use details that appeal to the senses: touch, sight, hearing, taste, and smell.

Personal Letter or E-mail

A personal letter is an informal message written to a friend or relative. While letter-writing was once an important way of communicating, more recently electronic mail (e-mail) has overtaken it as the most popular type of written correspondence. Both traditional and electronic letters have similar, although not identical, uses and conventions.

Purpose and Audience

Personal letters and e-mails are written for the purpose of keeping in touch, expressing thanks, or offering good wishes, congratulations, or greetings to people you know well. While e-mail is acceptable for short notes, keeping in touch, and urgent messages, letters or cards are still considered more acceptable for marking formal occasions such as births, deaths, illnesses, graduations, or for offering thanks.

Organization

- Organize a personal letter as if you were having a conversation. You can jump from subject to subject as long as you make some kind of connection between each topic.

  It felt great to win the art competition; I thought I was going to cry when they announced my name over the loudspeaker!

  Oh, and speaking of crying, have you seen that new Leo Di Caprio movie?…

Style

- If you are just writing to keep in touch with a friend, use a casual, friendly tone—try to make it sound as if you are speaking directly to the person reading the letter. Slang, colloquial language, and other non-standard expressions are acceptable as long as your reader will understand your meaning. For more serious occasions, when cards or a traditional letter is required, adopt a more formal tone and use conventional language. **See Colloquialisms and Slang, p. 95.**

- It can be helpful to use standard expressions (for example, "Sorry to hear that you are ill," "Thank you so much for the…," "Our thoughts and best wishes are with you on your graduation," "Our deepest condolences…," etc.) to mark occasions. However, be sure to personalize the letter by including an anecdote (a personal story or experience) related to the occasion or situation you are acknowledging, or by recalling a memory of the person, sharing your own feelings, describing how you plan to use the gift, and so on.

Format

Letters have a particular format. Although business and personal letters have different purposes and audiences, they both follow the same basic pattern, with some variations.

- **Return address:** This is sometimes left out of personal letters. In business letters, it may be preprinted on a letterhead.

- **Inside address:** This is the address of the person to whom you are writing. Note that there is no punctuation at the end of each line, and that the postal code is separated from the rest of the address by two spaces.

- **Date:** There are several ways of writing the date. In personal letters, it is common to write out the month and use a comma between the date and the year, rather than using numerals (for example, August 12, 1999 rather than 12/8/99), but both forms are acceptable.

Nadia Hajduk   [return address]
1873 34th Ave. SW
Calgary, AB R9V V4C

Rudi Corelli   [inside address]
365 Western Ave.
Millbrook, AB R6T Q1B

July 7, 2002   [date]

Dear Rudi,   [greeting]

Thanks so much for letting me stay with you last
month. It was a blast, and you really saved my skin.
If it hadn't been for your family offering to take
me in, I'd have had to miss graduation.

I'm slowly, slowly getting used to our new place. It's
only been a week since I arrived, but it feels like
ages, and I already miss you and the whole gang. I saw
the school I'll be going to next year; it's huge and
kind of scary, but it has a great track, and apparently
the gym teacher is really good, so I'm hoping to try out
for the team in the fall.

The new house is bigger than our old one (no more
sharing with my sister!), and I've got a view of the
street from my bedroom window. Mom says you can come   [body]
visit us later in the summer, if your parents say it's
OK. I can hardly wait.

By the way, did you notice I'm using the special paper
you gave me as a going-away present? It looks great,
huh? I expect to get a lot of use out of it this summer,
keeping in touch with you and everyone else back home.
(Home? Hmm. I guess I'll have to get used to calling
this place home now. I wouldn't mind if I could just
convince you and everyone else to move here with us!)

Well, gotta go. I'm going downtown to check out the
mall. Thanks again for putting up with me for the last
month of school. My mom is going to write and thank
your mom, too. Hope to see you SOON.

Love,   [closing]

Nadia   [signature]

P.S. My new address is at the top of the page.
Please write to me when you get a chance and   [postscript]
let me know what's happening.

- **Greeting:** Use a comma after the greeting in a personal letter (*Dear Manuel,*); use a colon in a business letter (*Dear Mr. Franchi:*).

- **Body:** Here is where you write what you want to say. Remember to break up your message into paragraphs to make it easier to read.

- **Closing:** If you are writing to a family member or a very close friend, you might close with *Love* or *Affectionately*; for other correspondents, consider one of the following complimentary closings:

Yours truly,	Sincerely,	Best regards,
Yours,	Sincerely yours,	Regards,

- **Signature:** Always sign a personal letter in your own handwriting, even if you use a computer to write it.

- **Postscript (P.S.):** Any afterthoughts or additional information can be included at the end of a personal letter after your signature and preceded by the abbreviation P.S.

Follow the same guidelines for e-mails as for traditional letters, with the following exceptions and additions:

- The return address on an e-mail is usually inserted automatically by your computer. If you are writing from someone else's computer, and want the person to respond to your home address, remember to include it in the body of your letter.

- The inside address is the e-mail address of the person you wish to reach. Remember to leave no spaces between names, and double-check that you have written it correctly, or your message will come back undelivered.

- The date (and time) will probably be inserted automatically by your e-mail program.

- Many people omit the salutation (greeting) in an e-mail, launching right into the body of the message. While this is acceptable for business e-mails, it is best to include some form of salutation in a personal message, either the standard "Dear so-and-so," or the more relaxed "Hi, So-and-so" followed by a comma.

- Keep the body of an e-mail fairly short. While personal letters may continue for pages, e-mails tend to be shorter (and sent more frequently).

- Finally, the complimentary close on a personal e-mail may be omitted (just key in your name at the bottom left margin, separated from the body by a line space) or you can use any of the letter closings suggested previously.

Business Letter or E-mail

A business letter or e-mail is any message you send to an individual (other than a friend or relative) or business in order to give or obtain information, buy or sell goods or services, or request that a particular action be taken.

Purpose and Audience

People write business letters to complain, request, order, give information, sell, or convince the reader to do something. Business letters are written to businesses or organizations, or to individuals whom the writer does not know well.

Organization

- State your reason for writing the letter in the first sentence, then follow up with background information, details, reasons, or examples.

- At the end of the letter, you should thank the person, and outline what action you would like him or her to take.

Style

- Use a courteous tone in a business letter, even if you are writing to complain about something.

- Business letters and e-mails use formal language and standard grammar, spelling, and punctuation.

- In business writing, say what you have to say directly and efficiently. Use short sentences and avoid any unnecessary words or expressions.

Format

The format of a business letter is the same as that of a personal letter, with these exceptions:

- If you are writing to a company but don't have the name of the person to whom the letter should be directed, use *Dear Sir or Madam*, or the person's title: *Dear Human Resources Manager*.

- Keep the body of the letter as brief as possible.

- Use one of the more formal closings listed on page 40.

- Type your name four lines beneath the closing, and put your handwritten signature in the space between these two elements.

There are several ways of setting up a traditional business letter. What follows are descriptions of two models. Either layout is acceptable for any business letter you wish to send.

- In **full block** style, you begin all lines at the left-hand margin and double-space between each element (for example, between the inside address and the date, between the date and the greeting, between paragraphs, etc.).

- In **modified block**, the return address, date, complimentary close, and your name and signature should begin at the centre of the page. All other lines begin at the left-hand margin. Use the same spacing as full block.

- If you are writing on paper that already has a letterhead, do not include a return address. Instead, write the date two lines below the letterhead, and then leave two to six lines before beginning the inside address.

What follows is a sample business letter, written in modified block.

Sheila Killin
St. Peter School
465 Westwood Road
St. Michael's, Ontario M6B 1Q9

15/4/01

Dr. Knute Janssen, Senior Analyst
Environment Canada
255 Front Street
St. Michael's, Ontario M6B 3G5

Dear Mr. Janssen:

I am writing to request a phone interview with you for a school project I am doing on the subject of greenhouse gases.

I am a Grade 9 student at St. Peter School, and I am preparing an oral report on the greenhouse effect for my science class. I have read your book and would be very interested in hearing your answers to some questions I have about this topic.

The interview will take about fifteen minutes of your time, and could take place whenever it is most convenient for you. My project is due on May 8, so I would appreciate an answer by May 1. You can reach me at my father's e-mail address: jkillin@here.com.

Thank you for your prompt reply.

Yours truly,

Sheila Killin

Sheila Killin

Research Report

A written research report presents facts, information, and sometimes opinions about a specific topic, based on research done by the writer.

Purpose and Audience

In school, the purposes of a report are usually twofold: first, to show your teacher that you have done adequate research on your topic (and that you have chosen a logical way of presenting it); and secondly, to present the information in a lively and interesting way to both your teacher and other students.

Organization

- A report should be organized logically, in a way that helps the reader follow what you are saying. For information reports you write in school, some common arrangements are listed below.

Arrangement of Information	Examples
by feature or characteristic	a report comparing two makes of computer a report that describes a new machine or invention
by time sequence	a report that looks at the history of Canada's involvement in the space program a report on the process of metamorphosis in insects
by order of importance (e.g., from most to least important, or from least to most important)	a report that examines the impact that a road will have on a wilderness area

- You may even use more than one kind of arrangement in the same report, as in the outline that follows (facing page). Note, however, that the overall organization in the example is by feature.

Topic: Skateboarding

Main Idea	Supporting Details
I. History of skateboarding	*arranged by time sequence*
II. Benefits of skateboarding	*has most important ideas at beginning and end of the section*
III. Safety precautions	*moves from most important to least important*
IV. Buying a skateboard	*arranged from the least important choice to the most important choice (the kind of skateboard being recommended)*

Style

- Reports are usually written in formal language using the third person (*he, she, they, it*).

- Try to adopt a factual, objective tone (that is, avoid words with strong good or bad connotations) that will convince your reader that the information you are presenting is trustworthy.

- Linking words that make connections between paragraphs and between sentences within paragraphs will help to make the report flow more smoothly, and clarify connections among ideas. **See Linking Words, p. 73.**

Format

- If your report is longer than two pages, add a cover page. Include the report title, your name, your teacher's name, and the due date. Check with your teacher to find out if she or he wants the information on the cover page arranged in a certain way.

- Headings can help make the information in your report easier to find. Set off headings using capital letters, boldfacing, italics, or underlining, and leave a line of space before and after.

- Give a source for all of the ideas and quotations you used from your research, and include a bibliography at the end of the report. **See Citations and Footnotes, p. 64; Bibliography, p. 67.**

Oral Report

An oral report is a report given out loud, in front of a group or an audience. While the content of an oral report may be similar to that of a written report, oral reports can be presented in different ways, using a variety of aids—such as computer graphics, slides, and working models—to help clarify or reinforce specific points. Some common forms of oral reports are speeches, demonstrations, and presentations.

Purpose and Audience

The purpose of an oral report is the same as that of a written report. The audience may consist of your classmates, your teacher, or both. Occasionally, you may be asked to present an oral report to another class or group. In business, oral reports are often presented to managers and other associates to give them a quick overview of a situation.

Organization

Oral reports are usually organized in the same way as written reports.

Style

• When you deliver an oral report, your listeners do not have a second chance to go back and reread if they miss something. To help them follow your presentation, therefore, provide clues that will lead them to anticipate what you are going to say. Here are some suggestions:

– Near the beginning of your presentation, state your thesis and give your audience an idea of how you will go about proving it. For example:

I believe that the wetlands must be saved, for three important reasons.

OR

The main stages in metamorphosis are egg, larva, pupa, and adult. I will describe each of these stages in turn.

- Use linking words such as *first, second, third,* etc. to connect paragraphs and ideas.

- Every so often, summarize what you have said and what remains to be said.

  So far, we have looked at the difference between the egg and the larva stage of metamorphosis. Now, we need to look at the last two stages in the process: pupa and adult.

• Repeat specific words or ideas several times throughout the presentation to reinforce key points.

• Don't try to include too much information in a single presentation. When possible, present your information in groups of threes: three sections, three reasons, three stages, etc. Grouping information in this way helps the audience to remember what you are saying.

• Use facial expressions, gestures, pauses, and changes in your tone of voice to draw attention to important points.

• Consider using slide shows, overheads, charts, or the chalkboard if they will help your audience to understand your ideas and make connections.

Science Report

Scientists write reports to document the results of experiments they have conducted. In fact, writing and publishing these results is a very important part of the process of acquiring scientific knowledge. Therefore, it is important that science reports are written clearly, and contain complete and accurate information.

Purpose and Audience

When scientists write up the results of their research, their purpose is to show their colleagues that the work has been done correctly and that the experiment could be repeated. The same expectations apply to reports you write in school: your teacher wants to see that you have understood the concepts, that you know how to apply them, and that you have done a thorough job.

Organization

Your science teacher may suggest a particular way that she or he would like you to organize your report. What follows is a common organizational pattern for science writing.

- **Problem:** This states the hypothesis (that is, what you expected to find out) and gives some background—usually arranged historically—on the problem or area of study, ending with the most recent theories or experiments that have been conducted.

- **Method:** This section includes a detailed description of how to perform the experiment or do the research. Include all the equipment needed, as well as information on when, where, and how to carry out the experiment, if relevant. You should include enough information here to allow someone else to perform the same experiment. Use a careful step-by-step arrangement in this part of your report.

- **Results:** Record your results without commenting on them. Include charts or graphs if these will help to make the information understandable. Present your results in whatever order seems logical (for example, from most important to least important).

- **Discussion:** Here is where you talk about what your results mean. Did they prove or disprove your hypothesis? Did anything go wrong? How can you explain any strange or odd findings? Do your results match those of other similar experiments or current research findings? It is usually best to organize the Discussion section in the same order in which you discuss your results. Or, if one point is of much more interest than another, use a most-important-to-least-important order.

Style

- Science writing is expository. You can offer explanations if things don't work out as you expected, and you can make judgments about what you think should happen, but do so in an unbiassed, objective manner. You are interested in the truth, not in being right.

- Avoid words with strong connotations (for example, don't refer to a chemical solution as "goo").

- Use correct terminology, and explain any terms with which your reader may not be familiar.

- Avoid trying to sound "scientific." There is no reason why science writing has to be overly formal or difficult to read. Present your information clearly, accurately, and simply.

- Connect your thoughts with linking words (such as *therefore*, *then*, and *in conclusion*).

- Use the passive voice when explaining experiments and other processes because it places more emphasis on what happened than on who did what. (However, use the active voice if you worked in a group and your teacher *wants* to know who did what.) **See Active and Passive Voice, p. 75.**

    First, 2 mg of sodium bicarbonate were measured and placed in a test tube. Then, 1 mg of vinegar was added using an eyedropper.

- Use headings (for example, *Problem*, *Method*, etc.) to separate the sections, and tables, graphs, or charts to present numerical information.

Sample Science Report

Monitoring Temperature Changes

Problem

Some doubt has been cast recently by a few scientists on long-standing procedures used to collect world temperature data in the past 100 years. Objections have been raised about the use of thermometers located at ground level near cities to monitor global temperatures. This method does not monitor the temperature in many areas of the globe. Would these areas of the Earth's surface reflect the same temperature changes as have been recorded over land surfaces?

The objections have been based on the assumption that different surfaces of the Earth, such as land, water, and forests, might respond differently to sunlight. Some surfaces might generate more heat than others and, therefore, increase the temperature of the atmosphere. These assumptions must be confirmed or refuted in response to the critics. If all the different surfaces of the Earth reflect the same amount of heat, then temperature data recorded over land would be the same as the atmosphere over water and forests.

Method

Three experiments will be conducted. Experiment A will involve a pan of water; Experiment B a pan of black soil; and Experiment C a pan of soil covered with leafy plants (see Diagram 1). The pans should be equal in size. Each pan should be placed in a closed paper box 18" x 12" x 12" [45 cm x 30 cm x 30 cm]. Tape a thermometer to the inside of each box. The front of the box should be cut open and closed off with a glass pane. Each box should be placed in the sunlight in a location where the temperature is approximately 20°C. The glass side of the box should face the sun. The sun should shine into each box for 120 min.

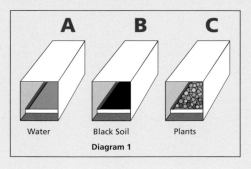

Diagram 1

Take the temperature in each box at the beginning of the 120-min. period and record it. Each box should record the same temperature—approximately 20°C. Take the temperature in each box at the end of the 120-min. period. Record the temperature for each experiment.

Results

Chart 1 (below) shows the results of these experiments.

Chart 1 Temperature Recordings		
Experiments	Start	Finish
A	20º	21.1º
B	20º	23.7º
C	20º	22.3º

The temperature in each of the boxes was different at the end of the experimental period. Experiment B recorded the highest temperature increase; Experiment A, the lowest increase. Experiment C was in between. This proves that black soil exposed to sunlight generates more heat than the other two surfaces.

Discussion

Before any conclusions can be drawn from this data, the experiments should be repeated several times. Other variables (i.e., time of day, type of box, etc.) should be checked to determine whether they might account for the difference in temperatures. If the results of this experiment check out, their implications should be explored. The critics of the ground level method for monitoring global temperatures may have a legitimate objection.

It now becomes important to check out the temperature variations that occur in the atmosphere over oceans, rain forests, and mountains so as to get an accurate record of global temperature changes. Since two-thirds of the Earth is covered by water and large areas of the land surface is covered by forests, the total atmosphere may not reflect the warming trend recorded over land. Steps should be taken to monitor temperature changes in the atmosphere over all types of the Earth's surface. This may require the use of alternative methods for monitoring global temperatures.

Essay

An essay presents a point of view on a topic. A **personal essay** explores a topic of interest to the writer, and tells something about the writer as well as the topic. In the more academic **formal essays**, which are a major part of most college and university programs, the focus is on gathering ideas or information and presenting them clearly and logically. Essays can be descriptive, persuasive, or expository.

Purpose and Audience

The purpose of an essay is to express a point of view about something. Essays written in school are usually written for a teacher or your classmates. Essays published in newsletters, newspapers, and magazines usually reflect the interests and opinions of the publication's readership.

Organization

Everything in an essay should support the thesis. In a tightly structured essay, every paragraph contains a topic sentence that is directly linked to the thesis, and every detail within the paragraph is directly linked to the topic sentence.

Just as the subject matter and style of an essay can vary greatly, so can the best method of organizing it. Here are some general guidelines:

- Persuasive essays work well if you begin and end with a strong argument, putting your weaker points in the middle. This approach is particularly effective if you expect that your audience will be hostile to your ideas.

- An essay in which you want to explore several options and then settle on a final solution may be organized from least important (the weakest option or argument) to most important (the solution or point of view you are proposing). Use this method for persuasive pieces if you think your audience is neutral or friendly to your cause.

- Other essays may move from feature to feature or from a general statement to specific examples.

Style

- Essays vary in style and tone, depending on the subject matter and purpose. (The sample essay that appears on the following pages is an example of a personal essay that makes a serious point.)

- Personal essays tend to be written in an informal style using the first person (*I, me*) or the third person (*he, she, they, it*).

- Academic or formal essays are written in formal language, using the third person.

- Supporting details are very important in an essay. Use examples, facts, anecdotes, evidence, quotations, logical arguments (*if this is true, then that must follow*), or whatever kind of support is most likely to impress your intended audience.

- Maintain a consistent tone throughout your essay. Do not start out writing an informal personal essay and then switch to a more formal tone halfway through.

Forms

Sample Essay

I remember a conversation with a producer who was working on turning one of my books into a feature film. The more I heard, the more I became convinced that I had better savour the moment when "Based on the Novel by..." flashed on the screen, because it was going to be the only thing in the movie even vaguely reminiscent of what I wrote.

I think it finally sank in when the producer said, "Well, you know the scene where Steve—?"

"Wait a second," I interrupted. "Who's Steve?"

How ignorant of me to think that, as the guy who wrote the book, I should actually be able to recognize the hero, especially after they plotted, replotted, unplotted, added, excised, and replaced personnel like Harold Ballard. Can't tell the players without a scorecard.

Then I thought of the junior high school student who might someday be called upon to do a book report on my book. He would plow over to the video store and rent *that* movie, save time, and come up with a report destined to flunk with flying colours. (The character sketch of Steve would lay a particularly large egg.) Every one of us has beaten a deadline by condensing a lot of reading time into a ninety-minute movie.

All this is hypothetical, of course, because the proposed movie never got made—which is why I am not dictating this piece over the cellular phone in my Maserati. But it did get me thinking about book versus movie, and what makes a book so special, since it obviously isn't time efficiency.

Lately, teachers have thrown us a curve. Now we have to read the book *and* see the movie, and compare the two. Teachers are very big on comparisons. Here it works. Almost invariably, the book gets the nod.

That's not to say that all the movies are bad. After the books, though, they're just somehow incomplete. The novel always seems to have something more—a greater depth, a different perspective, a more incisive insight and humour. There is something unique to the written word—to that relationship between author and reader—which cannot be reproduced any other way. It's more than just reporting or storytelling. It's *different.*

A reader participates in a novel. In a sense, it is almost a collaboration between him and the writer as, reading, he supplies his own interpretation—the reader's draft. No two are ever alike. You can read the same book as someone else without reading the same book.

(For instance, everybody who read *Lord Jim* and liked it read a different book than I did. That may be because I'm a poor "collaborator" with Joseph Conrad.) There is a feeling of accomplishment when you come to the end of a very good book—you have completed a successful collaboration. Don't expect royalties.

This is all coming from someone who was a staunch non-reader in elementary school. Once, in a book report, just to avoid actually reading anything, I went so far as to make up an entire novel, characters and all, using my friend's kid sister as the writer. There was even a section on "other books by the same author," and an excerpt from the *Boston Globe* review. It took ten times as much energy as doing the assignment properly, but to me, no amount of figuring the angles was unjustified. I didn't want to read, period. I got an A. Crime pays.

What finally hooked me in was humour. When I found books that made me laugh, my sense of the "work" of reading was replaced by something wonderful and totally unfamiliar—a desire to find what happened next. It was a crucial connection. From then on, I equated reading with enjoying myself, and I was a reader for good.

This may sound like an oversimplification, but beware. Relating reading and enjoyment can't be taught; it has to happen. It's a click. Without that click, no amount of explanation, no pleading, no assurance that this is a "great story," will do any good. In my case, humour produced the desired click. But mystery, suspense, adventure, science fiction, romance, and non-fiction can do the job too. I tend to stick with the funny stuff as the best bet. Tastes can be very specialized, but just about everybody loves to laugh.

My father used to summarize his reading history with the statement, "I read a book once," which was, unfortunately, not greatly exaggerated. Then, out of parental loyalty, he started reading my work. But when I didn't seem to be churning them out fast enough, he tried other authors, and found that you don't have to be a blood relative to appreciate good writing. Now it's not uncommon to find him with a good book in his hand. Reading helps you develop a facility for language, which in turn helps you to read. A neat circle....

from "Based on the Novel" by Gordon Korman

Research

3

Contents

3

Using the Library

Three important resources for finding information at the library are the **catalogue**, the **periodicals index**, and the **librarian**.

Catalogue

Every library has either a card catalogue or a computerized catalogue (or both). Each book in the catalogue is filed under at least three different headings: subject, title, and author. In computer files, you may also be able to search by contents, by key words, or in other ways. Your choices of search method will be listed on the main menu.

Use author and title searches when you know the specific book or author name you wish to find. Use a subject search when you are trying to narrow down your topic or find out what resources are available.

Start your search with the most specific word you can think of. For example, if you want to find information about the Canadian bush pilot Punch Dickins, try looking under "Dickins" first. If nothing comes up, broaden the search by typing in "bush pilots." If your results are still unsatisfactory, try "Canada—aviation."

Once you've found a book that seems suitable, write down the call number that is listed on the card or computer screen. The call number tells you where in the library the book is shelved. The letter R or REF before the number means it is a reference book and cannot be signed out; J or JUN probably means it's in the children's collection. If you are using a computerized catalogue, check to see if the system includes a brief description of the book or its table of contents, and whether or not the book is out on loan.

You will probably notice that most of the books in your subject area have similar call numbers. That is because the call numbers are arranged by general subjects. When you go to the shelf to find a book, take a moment to scan nearby titles. Often, you will find more interesting possibilities.

Here is a list of subjects and where to look for them:

Call No.	Subject
000–099	Generalities
100–199	Philosophy
200–299	Religion
300–399	Social Sciences
400–499	Language
500–599	Science
600–699	Technology
700–799	Fine Arts
800–899	Literature
900–999	History and Geography

Periodicals Index

A periodicals index is a list on CD-ROM or in print of recent newspaper and magazine articles. Some popular indexes are *The Canadian Business and Current Affairs Index* (CBCA) and the *Reader's Guide*. Ask the librarian to show you where the periodicals index is kept.

Like the catalogue, indexes are usually arranged by author, title, and subject. If you're using a CD-ROM data base, many of the articles listed will be available right there on screen; however, with a printed index, you have to check if the library carries that particular magazine or newspaper, and then find the issue yourself.

Newspaper and magazine articles are crucial resources if your topic is a current event or something that happened so recently that books about the subject have not yet been published.

Librarian

The librarian is arguably the best resource in the library. In addition to recommending useful books, librarians can help you find other resources and information that you may not have even considered, such as

- audiovisual material (tapes, videos, etc., which may or may not be listed in the catalogue)

- on-line data bases (e.g., encyclopedias or indexes on CD-ROM)

- vertical files (files of newspaper clippings, brochures, etc. on specific topics that are compiled and kept up-to-date by the librarians)

- government papers and publications

Internet Research

The Internet is another useful resource. Its sources tend to be more up-to-date than books or even periodicals, but beware! Since anyone can post information on a Web site, what you read is not always accurate. Double-check facts with at least one other source.

When you search for information on the Internet, you use a search engine instead of a catalogue or index. Yahoo, Alta Vista, and Excite are a few of the most popular search engines. If you can't find what you want with one search engine, try a different one.

As with the library computer catalogue, start your search by typing in the most specific key word or phrase you can think of. If you type a phrase into a search engine, put quotation marks around it; otherwise, the results will include all the Web pages that contain ANY ONE of the words. For example, typing *Canadian bush pilots* might produce pages on everything from Canadian unity to rose bushes. If you type the same phrase in quotation marks, you will get a list of only those pages that contain those three words together.

How do you decide which Web sites to visit from the list? First, eliminate those that obviously don't have much to do with what you want. Then, find more official-looking sites. Sites posted by individuals may be less trustworthy. You can tell something about a listed Web site by looking at the letters at the end of the address.

Address	Meaning
.ca	Canadian site
.com	business or company-run site
.edu	educational site
.gc.ca	Canadian government site
.gov	government (usually the U.S. government) site
.in	international organization site
.org	not-for-profit organization site (e.g., the United Way)
.net	network or Internet services site (e.g., service providers, search engines, etc.)

When you get to an actual Web site, scan the menu or map that lists the categories of information contained on that Web site. If it looks useful, bookmark it. If it doesn't seem suitable, see if it has a list of links to related sites; you may find something closer to what you need among these sites.

Avoid following every link on every page, though. Be selective, or you will soon find yourself confused and overloaded with information. One way to avoid getting sidetracked is to write your purpose or topic as a question—or series of questions—on a sticky note and post it on your computer (for example, "What role did Punch Dickins play in the opening of the North?"). Having your topic in sight and reading it every so often will help you to stay focussed.

Interviews

Interviews are a good way to get expert opinions or advice on a specific topic. It's usually best to schedule interviews after you have decided on a topic and done some research. That way, you can ask more meaningful and specific questions. What follows is a list of tips for handling interviews.

Before the interview…

- Decide how you will conduct the interview: by phone, by mail or e-mail, or in person. (Never arrange to meet an interviewee alone: pick a public place, such as an office or library, and bring a partner or an adult along with you.)

- Contact the person you want to interview and ask his or her permission. Be prepared to explain why you want to do the interview, what you expect to get out of it, when you need to have the information, and how much time it is likely to take. Let the interviewee choose a time that is convenient for him or her.

- Prepare a list of questions based on what you already know about the topic. Try to word your questions so that they cannot be answered with a simple *yes* or *no*.

Yes/No Questions	Open-Ended Questions
Did you meet bush pilots Punch Dickins and Wop May?	What were Punch Dickins and Wop May like?
Is it true that Wop May was almost shot down by the Red Baron in World War II?	Can you tell me something about Wop May's close call with the Red Baron?

- Start with some general or factual questions, and move on to more specific or in-depth issues once you are both comfortable.

- Arrive early for an interview; don't keep your guest waiting.

- Come prepared. You'll need a notepad, several pens or pencils (sharpened), your list of questions, and a tape recorder, if you have one available. (Note: If you plan to tape the interview, be sure to obtain the interviewee's permission to do so first, and take notes anyway; you may find some sections of the tape difficult to hear or understand.)

During the interview…

- Listen first, then take notes. If you don't understand an answer, try repeating in your own words what you think was said ("You mean,…"). If a new question occurs to you that you think would be useful for your research, ask it, but don't stray too far from the topic.

- Note down comments that might work well as direct quotations. Listen carefully for appropriate phrases or sentences and ask the interviewee to repeat them. Write down word-for-word what was said and then ask the interviewee to check what you wrote for accuracy.

- Be polite, not argumentative. At the end of the interview, thank the person for taking the time to speak with you.

- Watch the time. Try not to go over the time limit you estimated at the beginning by more than a few minutes.

After the interview…

- Review your notes right away. Add any words or explanatory notes, and rewrite any words that are difficult to read. If you absolutely must call the interviewee to clarify something, do so as soon as possible after the interview, and try to limit the number of questions.

- Listen to the tape recording, if you made one, and add to your notes any important information that you missed.

- Write a brief letter thanking the person for his or her co-operation.

Using Quotations

Here are some tips for using quotations in an essay or report:

- Beginning your paper with a quotation is a good way to grab the attention of your readers. Consult some dictionaries of quotations for ideas. You will find larger collections in the reference section of your library. Some smaller collections are available on the Internet, but remember to double-check them for accuracy whenever possible.

  Bartlett's Familiar Quotations is perhaps best known and a good resource for historical quotations from literature and poetry, but there are many other resources from which to choose. *Colombo's Canadian Quotations*, for example, contains quotations by Canadian politicians, celebrities, writers, and public figures on a variety of topics.

- Although you should write in your own words most of the time, a direct quotation from a reliable source (for example, an expert in a particular field) is a great way to support one of your ideas or arguments. Always credit the person whom you are quoting, set his or her words in quotations marks, and give a source for the quotation. **See Citations and Footnotes, below.**

- Be careful not to change the meaning of a quotation by taking parts of it out of context (that is, by using it in a way that was not intended). For example, if a movie reviewer sarcastically calls a movie "the most exciting action picture since *The Sound of Music*," it would be unfair to quote him or her as saying the movie was a "most exciting action picture."

Citations and Footnotes

In essays and research papers, either include citations right in the body of the text or add footnotes at the bottom of the page to list the sources of quotations, charts, tables, diagrams, and all ideas other than your own.

Citations

What follows are some general guidelines for writing citations.

- Place the author's name and the page number(s), if appropriate, in parentheses after the borrowed material. If the citation is at the end of a sentence, the period should follow the citation.

  > "The Arctic is mostly water—with ice on top, of course—and that ice is never more than a few feet thick" (Armstrong 7).

- If what you have written tells readers which author you are crediting, you don't need to repeat that author's name in the citation.

  > According to Jennifer Armstrong, "The Arctic is mostly water—with ice on top, of course—and that ice is never more than a few feet thick" (7).

  > As Teri Degler reminds us, "Even if the average temperature went up only 10°C, some of the ice at the North and South poles might melt and raise the level of the oceans" (15), which would be catastrophic for low-lying countries like Bangladesh.

- If you have referred to more than one work by the same author in your paper, include a shortened version of the title. For example, if you mentioned two of Alice Munro's short stories in a paper—perhaps "Miles City, Montana" and "Jesse and Meribeth"—you could refer to (Munro, "Miles" 119) or (Munro, "Jesse" 249) in your citations.

Footnotes

For footnotes, instead of placing information in the text, put a small raised number at the end of the borrowed material, and a footnote with the same raised number at the bottom of the page, separated from the text by a short line (about ten spaces long). Indent the first line of the footnote. Here is an example:

> "The Arctic is mostly water—with ice on top, of course—and that ice is never more than a few feet thick."[1]
>
> _____
>
> [1] Jennifer Armstrong, *Shipwreck at the Bottom of the World: The Extraordinary True Story of Shackleton and The Endurance* (New York: Crown, 1998) 7.

The first time you cite a source, give the full reference. For all subsequent references, cite only the author's last name and the page number.

[2] Armstrong 22.

Here are some other sample footnote references:

- **book with more than one author**

    [3] Ann-Maureen Owens and Jane Yealland, *Canada's Maple Leaf: The Story of Our Flag* (Toronto: Kids Can Press, 1999) 5–6.

- **work in an anthology**

    [4] Duke Redbird, "I Am a Canadian," *An Anthology of Canadian Native Literature in English*, eds. Daniel David Moses and Terry Goldie, 2nd ed. (Toronto: Oxford University Press, 1998) 120.

- **magazine**

    [5] David Jarzen, "Pollen Power," *Owl*, Mar. 1997: 12.

- **newspaper article**

    [6] Réal Gross, "Slug Found in Milk Bottle," *The Middleton Mercury*, 15 Oct. 2000: A1.

- **video or film**

  [7] Ole Gjerstad and Martin Kreelak, dir., *Journey to Nunavut: The Kreelak Story*, National Film Board of Canada, 1999.

- **CD-ROM**

  [8] "Film Animation," *The Canadian Encyclopedia*, World ed., CD-ROM (Toronto: McLelland & Stewart, 1996).

- **Internet text selection**

  Include the Web site's address and the date that you accessed the information.

  [9] "Communities Use Radar Satellite to Gauge Ice Breakup," *Nunatsiaq News*, Internet, 14 May 1999: http://www.nunatsiaq.com.

- **interview**

  [10] T. Jai Singh, personal interview, 10 March 2000.

Bibliography

A bibliography is a list of all the works consulted during the preparation of an essay or research paper. It should appear on a separate page at the end of the paper. Although styles vary, all bibliographies include the same basic information: the name of the author(s), the title of the work, and the name, date, and place of publication. (Note: If there is no author name given, start with the title of the work.) Indent all lines except the first line of each entry. Arrange the sources alphabetically, by author surname. Your teacher may have a particular style that he or she prefers. If not, some examples of bibliographical references appear on the following pages.

- **book with one author**

> Armstrong, Jennifer. *Shipwreck at the Bottom of the World: The Extraordinary True Story of Shackleton and* The Endurance. New York: Crown, 1998.

- **book with more than one author**

> Owens, Ann-Maureen, and Jane Yealland, *Canada's Maple Leaf: The Story of Our Flag.* Toronto: Kids Can Press, 1999.

- **work in an anthology**

> Redbird, Duke. "I Am a Canadian," *An Anthology of Canadian Native Literature in English*, eds. Daniel David Moses and Terry Goldie, 2nd ed. Toronto: Oxford University Press, 1998. 120.

- **magazine**

Place the volume number, if there is one, after the title of the magazine. Place the page numbers, preceded by a colon, at the end of the citation.

> Jarzen, David. "Pollen Power." *Owl* Mar. 1997: 12–14.

- **newspaper article**

As with the magazine citation, place the page numbers, preceded by a colon, at the end.

> Gross, Réal. "Slug Found in Milk Bottle." *The Middleton Mercury* 15 Oct. 2000: A1.

- **video or film**

> Gjerstad, Ole, and Martin Kreelak, dir. *Journey to Nunavut: The Kreelak Story.* National Film Board of Canada, 1999.

- **CD-ROM**

    The Canadian Encyclopedia. World ed. CD-ROM. Toronto:
    McClelland & Stewart, 1996.

- **Internet text selection**

    Include the Web site's address and the date you accessed the text.
    If you have publication information for the print version, include
    that after the title.

    "Communities Use Radar Satellite to Gauge Ice Breakup."
    Nunatsiaq News. 14 May 1999. Internet.
    http://www.nunatsiaq.com.

- **interview**

    Singh, T. Jai. Personal interview. 10 March 2000.

Plagiarism

Plagiarism is presenting the ideas of others as if they were your own.
It is against the law. To avoid plagiarism, be sure to include a citation
or footnote whenever you borrow ideas or quote directly from
another source. **See Citations and Footnotes, p. 64.**

Style

Contents

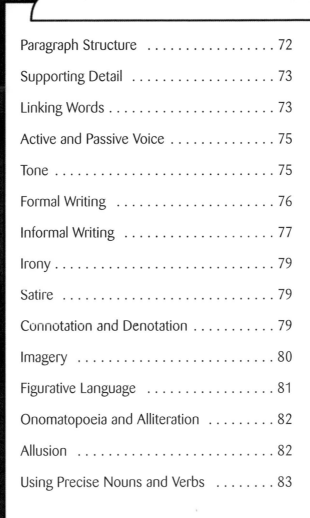

4

Paragraph Structure

A paragraph is a group of sentences that develop one phase of a narrative or descriptive piece, or one idea in an expository or persuasive piece. Paragraphs are well developed if they are unified, coherent, and complete.

A paragraph is **unified** if all the sentences in it relate to the same idea. The best way to make sure your paragraphs are unified is to start each one with a topic sentence that states the idea you are developing. Then make sure that all the sentences that follow clearly relate to the topic sentence. Here is an example:

> The once-proud Canadian Football League has had to face some major challenges in recent years. First, it lost many fans to baseball when teams were formed in Montreal and Toronto in the 1970s. Still more fans abandoned the game when new cable channels devoted to sports made live broadcasts of American football games widely available to people, and in the comfort of their own homes. Suddenly, the CFL, which once played to sold-out stadiums, was in danger of collapse.

To make a paragraph **coherent**, arrange the sentences in a clear and logical order, using linking words to show how they are related. **See Linking Words, p. 73.** You may want to start with a sentence that links the paragraph with the one before (called a *transition sentence*). Try to put the topic sentence near the beginning of the paragraph, followed by the supporting sentences arranged in a logical order.

When is a paragraph **complete**? It is complete when you have adequately supported the topic sentence. In the CFL example above, the two supporting points clearly back up the topic sentence, and show that the CFL faced some major challenges. The writer has mentioned the major challenges and has explained enough about what those challenges were, and how they affected the CFL, to make them understandable to the reader. So, the paragraph may be considered complete.

As a rule, it will take you between three and seven sentences to accomplish this goal. If your paragraph is longer than seven or so sentences, either separate those sentences into two paragraphs, or ask yourself if all that detail is necessary (sometimes it is). If it is shorter than three sentences, you probably haven't included enough information to cover the idea. Try joining the sentences to the paragraph before or after, or adding more detail. The exception to this general guideline is news stories, which often contain single-sentence paragraphs.

Supporting Detail

When you write an expository or persuasive piece, you'll need to back up your thesis with at least three main points. Each main point needs to be supported by details. There are many ways to support your main points. You might, for example, use

- facts
- statistics
- examples
- quotations from experts
- definitions

- anecdotes
- logical arguments
- steps in a sequence or process
- comparisons
- features

Linking Words

Linking words (also called *transition words*) show the relationship between sentences or paragraphs. Some common linking words are given in the chart on the next page.

For...	Try these linking words...	
Cause–Effect	as a result because consequently for this (these) reason(s)	however since therefore thus
Comparison/Contrast	although by contrast compared with (to) even though however	in the same way likewise on the other hand similarly
Conclusion	finally in conclusion in short in summary then	therefore to conclude to summarize to sum up
Emphasis	again also equally important furthermore	in addition in fact moreover
Explanation	because for example for instance for this (these) reason(s) furthermore	in addition in other words in particular since specifically
Importance	equally important finally first (second, third)	lastly most importantly next
Space/Location	ahead around behind below beside beyond inside	near next to on the left/right on top outside toward underneath
Time	after afterward as at last before during finally just then later	meanwhile next once since soon suddenly then while

Active and Passive Voice

A verb is in the active voice if its subject is the doer of the action. A verb is in the passive voice (*be* + past participle) when the subject of the verb receives the action.

Active: The firefighters extinguished the fire.
Passive: The fire was extinguished.

The passive voice allows the doer of the action to be left out when his or her involvement is unknown, unimportant, or obvious. Writers of scientific papers usually prefer the passive voice (for example, *The experiment was conducted...*).

Generally speaking, though, use the active voice whenever possible. It uses fewer words and is more precise.

Tone

Whatever you are writing, it is important to pay attention not only to *what* you say, but to *how* you say it—the tone. Tone is how the writer conveys his or her attitude to what she or he writes. When we speak, we convey our attitude by varying our tone of voice, facial expressions, and mannerisms. For example, we might frown, shake our fist, and raise our voice to show that we are angry. Writers use different means of expressing tone; word connotations, sentence length, rhythm, irony, repetition of key phrases, even punctuation can help to get across a particular attitude. The tone of a piece of writing can be formal or informal, enthusiastic, thoughtful, sarcastic, angry, passionate or objective, among others. Be careful to adopt a tone that suits your topic and your audience.

The notes that appear on the next page were written by the same person, but the tone of each varies from friendly, to angry, to amused.

Hi, neighbour! [friendly]

My name is Lynn, and I've just moved into unit 18B. I've been assigned parking space #67 for my car, which I guess you've been using up to now for your trailer. Sorry to bother you, but would you mind terribly moving it from there, so I can park? Perhaps you could put it in one of the other free spots farther up the street. (I notice there is one out-side Unit 12 that is almost never used.) Looking forward to meeting you in person soon! Oh, and I'd be happy to help get it hitched, if you would like.

Mr. Jones: [angry]

It's been a week, and that disgusting old trailer is still in my parking spot. Last night I was ticketed for parking on the street. Get it out of there immediately, or I'll have it towed.

Darling, [amused]

Do you remember when we first met, how upset I got about that old trailer of yours being in my parking space? It all seems so silly now. What in the *world* was I so upset about? Remember I called it a "disgusting old trailer"? (I certainly had a way with words, didn't I!) Anyway, the joke's on me; instead of helping you to hitch your trailer, I got hitched to you (and I couldn't be happier)! Isn't life strange?

Formal Writing

Formal writing is the writing style used for business letters, official documents, essays, and reports. **See Forms, p. 18.** Some points to remember when you are writing something with a formal tone appear on the facing page.

- In formal writing, the writer tends to be in the background. Use the first person (*I* or *me*) when it makes sense to do so, but keep your focus on the issue at hand rather than on yourself.

- Choose words that are familiar and generally accepted, not colloquialisms or slang.

- Carefully follow the conventions of grammar, avoiding the errors that are often accepted in casual spoken English (and sometimes in informal writing), such as sentence fragments, improper use of pronouns, and faulty subject–verb agreement.

- Do not use shorthand or shortcuts. Use only the most generally accepted abbreviations, and avoid the use of contractions (*can't*, *won't*, *isn't*, etc.). Unless your topic requires you to write a lot of numbers, spell out all numbers to ninety-nine.

- Use a colon between an introductory sentence and a quotation, or for the salutation in a formal business letter, and carefully follow the conventions for using commas and other punctuation.

- Try to create a smooth, even rhythm by choosing words carefully and varying sentence structures and lengths.

- Formal language does not have to be overly wordy, nor does it have to sound "official." You can write plainly and still make your writing formal enough for others to take it seriously.

  Overly wordy: Players should refrain from revealing their cards to other players until such time as they are called upon to do so.

  Formal but plain: Do not show your cards to other players until you are asked to do so.

Informal Writing

Informal writing is the kind of writing you might use to write a note to your friend or a close relative. It is writing that, to one degree or another, reflects the way people talk. Novelists and playwrights use informal language in dialogue to make their characters sound more true-to-life.

Writing can be more or less formal; the degree of formality you choose depends on what you are writing, to whom you are writing, and why you are writing. Most writing contains at least some informal elements. Some signs that writing is less formal include the following:

- It uses shortcuts: contractions (*can't, isn't,* etc.), abbreviations such as *e.g.* or *i.e.*, and, on occasion, sentence fragments.

- It uses colloquial or slang expressions. **See Colloquialisms and Slang, p. 95.**

- It has the rhythm and tone of someone talking out loud to a friend.

- Grammar and punctuation conventions are sometimes changed to suit the style or tone of the writing. For example, commas may be omitted; *they* or *their* might be used in place of a singular pronoun; sentence fragments may be used to make the writing sound more like conversation; and, in very informal writing, double negatives, slang words, or other non-standard forms of expression may be used to create a casual tone.

Here are some guidelines for informal writing:

- Use language that suits the occasion and the reader. You *can* use colloquial expressions and even slang, but that doesn't mean you *should*. A thank-you letter to your dear Aunt Sophia would not (and should not) sound the same as a quick note written to a school friend, although both would probably be written informally.

- Write clearly and simply. Try not to get so carried away with charming expressions or trendy language that you make it difficult for your reader to understand what you are saying; or worse, that you forget to say anything at all.

- Treat your readers with respect. If you are writing for a younger audience, or for readers who know less about a subject than you do, choose words that they will understand.

Irony

Irony occurs when a statement or situation means something different from (or even the opposite of) what is expected. For example, it would be ironic if someone who complained bitterly for years about a neighbour were saved by that neighbour during a house fire.

Another kind of irony is called **dramatic irony**. It occurs in plays when the audience knows something that the characters do not. The effect of dramatic irony can be funny (as when a character on stage is being made fun of behind his or her back), but it can also be tragic. For example, in the final act of *Romeo and Juliet*, the audience knows that Juliet is not really dead, but has simply taken a sleeping potion to make her appear so. When Shakespeare has Romeo find Juliet's seemingly lifeless body and kill himself from grief, he is using dramatic irony to heighten the sense of tragedy.

Satire

Satire uses humour, especially irony and sarcasm, to expose flaws or criticize someone or something. Usually, the purpose of satire is to point out weaknesses or foolish ideas. Writers, political cartoonists, and stand-up comedians often use satire to criticize society or government policies.

Connotation and Denotation

The definition of a word that you find in a dictionary is its **denotation**. Many words also have **connotations**, however. This means that they have positive or negative associations, or a particular mood or slant of meaning, that affect what the word tells the reader. For example, the words *giggle*, *laugh*, *guffaw*, *titter*, *chortle*, and *snicker* all denote more or less the same thing, but each has a different shade of meaning. Similarly, the adjective *careful* has a different connotation from *timid*. (How would *you* rather be described: as a careful person, or a timid one?)

Being aware of the positive or negative connotations of your words allows you to create sympathy for a character, set a mood, gain acceptance for your views, and control, or at least influence, the reactions of your readers.

Imagery

Imagery is the pictures or impressions that writers create in the mind of their readers. To create these impressions, they use descriptive techniques such as figures of speech (simile, metaphor, personification, oxymoron), onomatopoeia, alliteration, or allusions. Well-chosen nouns, verbs, and modifiers on their own can also create images. The following poem, for example, creates striking imagery by using simple yet powerful words.

The Red Wheelbarrow
by William Carlos Williams

so much depends
upon

a red wheel
barrow

glazed with rain
water

beside the white
chickens.

Figurative Language

Language can be literal or figurative. Literal language says what it means directly. Figurative language, on the other hand, uses words to paint a picture, draw an interesting comparison, or create a poetic impression. It uses words beyond their literal meanings to give added force or beauty to the effect they create. Some forms of figurative language are shown in the chart that follows.

Device	Definition	Example
Simile	Compares two things or ideas directly, using *like* or *as*	*His eyes gleamed like a pair of bright new pennies.*
Metaphor	An indirect comparison, without using *like* or *as*	*Her words pierced my heart.* (compares "her words" to the action of a knife or sword)
Personification	Attributing human qualities to an idea, thing, or animal	*The sun smiled down on us.*
Symbol	An object or person that represents a quality, idea, or condition. Some symbols are generally accepted, or even universal; others are used in specific stories or poems to mean specific things.	(e.g., Water is a universal symbol of both life and death.)
Oxymoron	A combination of contradictory words that create a striking effect	*fiery ice; an intelligent fool; joyful melancholy*
Hyperbole	A deliberately exaggerated statement made for effect	*My parents, who were sitting on the beach, seemed a thousand miles away.*

Onomatopoeia and Alliteration

Writers—especially poets and writers of fiction—often choose words for the way they sound as well as for their meaning. **Onomatopoeic words** are words that imitate actual sounds: *hiss, thud, crash, hush,* and *twitter* are some examples. **Alliteration** is the repetition of the same consonant sound in words that are close together to create an effect. For example, *the soft, sibilant sound of the wind whistling through the willows* creates a feeling of peace and tranquillity by repeating the sounds *s* and *w*. Both of these techniques can help to make your writing more lively and expressive.

Allusion

An allusion is a brief reference within a work of art to another character, place, event, or work of art. For example, a writer may allude to a well-known myth or legendary figure as a way of adding meaning to his or her own work. Saying that someone has a "Midas touch" is an allusion to the legend of King Midas, who turned everything he touched to gold.

Allusions can also refer to historical events, religious symbols, literary works, or even movies. A director of horror or suspense films, for example, might allude to the work of famous film director Alfred Hitchcock by imitating some of the unusual camera angles for which Hitchcock was famous.

Using Precise Nouns and Verbs

Nouns and verbs are the backbone of good writing. Whenever possible, use strong, concrete, specific nouns, and vivid, precise, energetic verbs.

> **Weak:** A nice smell of apple dumplings was in the air.
> **Stronger:** The aroma of apple dumplings wafted by.

Aroma is stronger and more precise than *nice smell*, and *wafted* is a far more striking verb than *was*, which requires a whole phrase (*in the air*) to support it.

Word Use

5

Contents

5

Using a Dictionary and a Thesaurus

A dictionary and a thesaurus are two tools that can help you use words more precisely. A **dictionary** provides some or all of the following information:

- word meanings

- spelling

- irregular forms of verbs (e.g., *bring/brought*), adjectives (e.g., *good/better/best*), and nouns (e.g., *child/children*)

- guidelines for using the word (these may be presented in boxes or notes near the entry, or in the entry itself)

- synonyms, antonyms, and/or homophones

- word origins (etymology)

A **thesaurus** contains a list of words and expressions that have similar or related meanings. Some thesauri also list words and expressions that mean the opposite of the word you are looking up.

A thesaurus offers more synonyms for a word than a dictionary does, but it is important to look up unfamiliar words or expressions in the dictionary to check that they have the meaning you intend. For example, if you look up the adjective *big* in a thesaurus, you'll find the words *great, large, considerable, fair, above par, massive, huge, ample, abundant, vast, immense, enormous*, and many others. While all of these words mean "big," they can't be used interchangeably in all situations. You would not say "He had an abundant nose," for example, but you might say "He had a large nose."

Prefix

A prefix is a word or syllable added on to the beginning of another word to change its meaning. For example, the prefix *dis-* added to the word *appear* makes *disappear*. Often, knowing what a prefix means can help you to figure out the meaning of a new word. What follows is a list of some common prefixes and their meanings.

Prefix (Meaning)	Example	Prefix (Meaning)	Example
ante- (before)	*antedate*	**mono-** (one)	*monotone*
anti- (against)	*antifreeze*	**multi-** (many)	*multicultural*
bi- (two)	*bicycle*	**non-** (not)	*non-stop*
co- (together)	*co-operate*	**post-** (after)	*postdate*
dis- (not)	*distrust*	**re-** (again)	*review*
extra- (beyond)	*extraordinary*	**retro-** (back)	*retro-rocket*
fore- (before)	*foreword*	**semi-** (half)	*semicircle*
hyper- (excessively)	*hypersensitive*	**super-** (beyond; over)	*supernatural*
in- (not)	*inactive*	**trans-** (across)	*transatlantic*
inter- (between; among)	*interlock*	**tri-** (three)	*triangle*
mal- (bad)	*malpractice*	**un-** (not)	*undecided*
mis- (wrong)	*misspell*	**uni-** (one)	*unicycle*

Word Use

Suffix

A suffix is a syllable or letters added to the end of a word to form another word. Often, adding a suffix can change a word from one part of speech to another. For example, if you add the suffix *-tion* to the verb *subtract*, it forms a noun (*subtraction*).

Even when a suffix doesn't create a new part of speech, it can add new meaning. Think of the difference between a concrete noun like *child* and an abstract noun like *childhood*, for example. Verbs often use suffixes such as *-ed* or *-ing* to help create different tenses: *I walk; I walked; I am walking*. Similarly, adding the suffixes *-er* or *-est* to some adjectives and adverbs forms the comparative (*faster, sooner*) and superlative (*fastest, soonest*).

The following chart shows some common suffixes along with their meanings. As you can see from the examples in the chart, adding a suffix sometimes requires a change in the spelling of the base word. **See Spelling Tips, p. 94**.

Suffix	Meaning	Example
-able; -ible	able suitable for inclining toward deserving to be that can be	*obtainable* *comfortable* *peaceable* *lovable* *edible; resistible*
-ate	having the quality or form of cause to be	*compassionate* *alienate*
-dom	position, realm, condition	*kingdom* *martyrdom*
-ed	having in the past/past participle	*bearded* *landed*
-ee	a person who is	*employee*

Suffix	Meaning	Example
-er; -or	a person or thing that more	*employer; instructor* *harder*
-ful	full of	*beautiful*
-hood	state or condition	*parenthood*
-ish	somewhat or near resembling belonging to	*youngish* *childish* *British*
-ism	practice system quality condition	*baptism* *capitalism* *heroism* *alcoholism*
-ize	make become	*legalize* *crystallize*
-less	without	*homeless*
-ly	in a certain manner like	*lightly* *ghostly*
-ment	act or state of	*enjoyment*
-ous	full of	*joyous*
-ship	position of power or skill of relation between	*kingship* *leadership* *partnership*
-sion; -tion	act, process, or condition of	*division* *exhaustion*
-ward	in a direction or to a point in time	*seaward* *upward*
-y	inclined to full of	*chatty* *juicy*

Word Use

Homophone

Homophones are words that are pronounced the same but have different meanings and, usually, spellings, such as *see* and *sea*. Many of the words listed under Commonly Confused Words (facing page) are homophones. Pay particular attention to words that have homophones when you are proofreading; they are easy to misspell. Some of the most common homophones are as follows:

hear/here	their/there/they're
it's/its	threw/through
passed/past	to/too/two
peace/piece	who's/whose
principal/principle	your/you're

Synonym

Synonyms are words that have similar definitions. For example, *discuss*, *talk*, and *chat* can all be said to mean more or less the same thing, but each has a different use, or connotation. **See Connotation and Denotation, p. 79.**

The council *discussed* the proposal at length.

The police officer *talked* to our class about bicycle safety.

Eli *chatted* to me on the phone.

Antonym

Antonyms are pairs of words with opposite meanings, such as *good/bad*, *stop/go*, *big/little*. Writers and speakers often use antonyms to highlight an idea or make a phrase stand out. For example, English author Charles Dickens began his novel *A Tale of Two Cities* with these famous words:

> It was the *best* of times, it was the *worst* of times.…

You will probably notice many other examples of antonyms in stories and essays you read. Try using them in your own writing.

Commonly Confused Words

The following list of commonly confused words contains some word pairs or triplets that are often confused because they sound the same (e.g., *your/you're*). Others seem to be related but have different uses (e.g., *accept/except*). Still others express similar meanings, but are used in different contexts (e.g., *among/between*). Study the list and take careful note of the words that you are most likely to confuse. Make it a habit to check your use of these words whenever you write.

accept means "agree to": *I accept your apology.*
except means "not including": *They all went on the trip except me.*

advice is a noun meaning "counsel": *My advice to you is be careful.*
advise is a verb meaning "counsel": *I advise you to be careful.*

all ready means "completely ready": *We are all ready to go.*
already means "before this time": *We are already on our way.*

alternate means "by turns" or "every other": *We have science on alternate days.*
alternative means "another choice": *The only alternative to this plan is to surrender.*

among is used for more than two: *Only one among the three of us wore glasses.*
between is used for two only: *We had only one match between the two of us.*

amount is for quantities that can't be counted: *A small amount of the gas escaped.*

number is for quantities that can be counted: *A small number of rats escaped from the lab.*

anyway is correct: *Anyway, I'll see you later.*

anyways is incorrect

bad is an adjective: *I feel bad about what I said.*

badly is an adverb: *I sing badly.*

complement means "something that completes": *Music is the perfect complement to a good meal.*

compliment means "praise": *Let me compliment you on winning first prize.*

could/should/would are sometimes followed by *have* or *'ve*, but never *of*: *I could've been hurt! You should have seen it fly.*

desert means a dry place: *the Sahara Desert*

dessert means something sweet eaten after a meal: *Apple pie is my favourite dessert.*

emigrate means "move from somewhere": *They emigrated from Iran.*

immigrate means "move to somewhere": *They immigrated to Canada.*

fewer is for quantities that can be counted: *I have fewer jellybeans than you do.*

less is for quantities that can't be counted: *I have less juice than she does.*

good is an adjective meaning "all right": *I feel good about winning the game.*

well is an adjective meaning "in good health" or an adverb meaning "in a favourable manner": *I have been well since I got over the flu. I did well on the test.*

hear means "listen to": *I hear what you are saying.*

here means "in this place": *The chair goes over here.*

it's means "it is": *It's raining outside.*
its means "belonging to it": *The hamster is cleaning its fur.*

lie means "to recline": *Lie down for a minute and rest.*
lay means "to put": *Lay your books down on the desk.* It is also the
    past tense of lie: *He lay down for a minute, and then fell asleep.*

loose means "not tight": *The knot came loose.*
lose means "to misplace": *Don't lose your book!*

passed is the past tense of "pass": *I passed the test.*
past is a noun meaning "a time before": *In the past, people had to
    make their own clothing.*

peace means "tranquillity": *A sense of peace flowed through me.*
piece means "segment": *Can I have a piece of that butter tart?*

principal means "first in importance": *"The principal reason for your good
    marks is that you studied hard," said the principal of the school.*
principle means "fact": *The principle of gravity explains why we fall
    down instead of up.*

regardless is correct: *I will go, regardless of what you say.*
irregardless is incorrect

set means "put": *Set the box over there.*
sit means "to be seated": *Sit on the chair.*

stationary means "not moving": *The train is stationary in the station.*
stationery means "writing paper": *I will write a letter on my new stationery.*

than is used for comparisons: *My hat is funnier than yours.*
then is an adverb meaning "at that time": *Just then, the balloon popped.*

their means "belonging to them": *We stayed in their house.*
there means "in or at that place": *Please stack the chairs over there.*
they're means "they are": *They're coming home today.*

threw means "hurled": *He threw the ball.*
through means "from end to end": *It went through the window.*

to is a preposition meaning "in the direction of": *Let's go to the party.*
too is an adverb meaning "excessively": *This chili is too spicy.*
two is an adjective meaning "the number after one": *I have two sisters.*

weather means "conditions outside": *This dry weather is not good for the crops.*
whether means "if": *We aren't sure whether we will have any corn.*

whose means "belonging to whom": *Whose is this jacket?*
who's means "who is": *Who's going to the movie?*
who's means "who has": *Who's got my pen?*

your means belonging to you: *Don't forget your bag.*
you're means "you are": *You're going to be late.*

Spelling Tips

Here are some tips to help you to avoid spelling errors in your work:

- **Trust your instincts.** If a word doesn't look right, it probably isn't.

- **Look for within-word patterns.** It is useful to relate patterns to word families; for example, *o-u-l-d* applies to *could*, *should*, and *would*.

- **Write it out.** If you aren't sure of the spelling of a word, try writing it out on paper several different ways until you find one that looks right.

- **Break it down.** Divide new or unfamiliar words into syllables, and listen for familiar prefixes, roots, and suffixes.

- **Look it up.** If you still aren't sure of the spelling, look up the word in a dictionary.

- **Learn from your mistakes.** Devise memory tricks to help you remember difficult words. For example, make up a rhyme or phrase (for example, *two helpings of dessert* may help you remember to use two s's in this word), or look for a smaller word inside a bigger word

(for example, *dent* in *independent; cry* in *crystal; age* in *manageable*).
Keep a personal list of words that you tend to misspell and refer to
it often.

When you are proofreading, remember that computer spell checkers
don't catch homophone errors. Use a spell-checking program if you
wish, but always proofread your work.

Colloquialisms and Slang

Colloquialisms are words or expressions that we use in everyday speech
or informal writing, but that aren't appropriate in more formal writing.
When you write essays or reports for school, you need to be aware
of the colloquialisms you use, and find alternative expressions when
necessary. Some examples of colloquial expressions (and some
alternatives) follow.

Colloquial Expression	Formal Alternative
Give me a break!	Don't bother me. OR Don't try to fool me.
No way!	That cannot be true.
hanging out	keeping company with OR spending time with
tooling around	walking around OR driving around
kidding	joking
You're pulling my leg!	You must be joking!

Slang is very informal language that is invented or used in a particular
way by a specific group and is rarely understood by those outside the
group. For example, teenagers often develop their own slang expressions
to use among themselves. Examples of slang from an earlier time

include *razzmatazz* and *tripping the light fantastic*. More recent slang expressions include *cool* for good, *get the boot* for losing a job, and *bummer* for a bad experience.

Slang is rarely used in informal writing because it goes out of date so quickly. Although slang may be appropriate in some advertisements, or in writing aimed at an audience of your peers, avoid using it in most writing you do for school assignments.

Jargon

Jargon is language that does not communicate. Writing that uses big, hard-to-understand words where a smaller word would do is often written off as jargon. So is writing that uses too many technical terms with which the reader is unfamiliar. If you are writing to a skateboarding friend about *ollies*, *180s*, and *kickflips*, he or she will have no trouble understanding what you mean; use those same terms in a letter to your grandmother, and you may be accused of using jargon.

Cliché

Clichés are overworked expressions that no longer have much impact. It's best to avoid using them in your writing. Here are some examples:

- free as a bird
- sick as a dog
- between a rock and a hard place
- last but not least
- in the home stretch
- under the weather

Euphemism

A euphemism is a word or expression that is meant to soften the impact of words or phrases that may be considered harsh or unpleasant. Here are some common euphemisms:

pass away   senior citizen   rest room   special needs

Euphemisms can be useful in some situations, but there can be a fine line between using a euphemism and covering up the truth. As a general rule, the direct way to say something is usually best.

Redundancy

Redundancy in writing is the use of unnecessary words.

Redundant: I woke up at 7:30 a.m. in the morning.
Better: I woke up at 7:30 a.m.

Redundant: The reason I stayed home is because I was sick.
Better: I stayed home because I was sick.

Redundant: That area is restricted and not everyone is allowed in there.
Better: That area is restricted.

Racist Language

Racist language is any language that refers to a particular cultural or ethnic group in insulting terms. But racism also exists in more subtle forms. Here are some guidelines for avoiding racism in your writing:

- Mention a person's race only if that is relevant to the context. If a person's race or ethnic origin *is* relevant, be as specific as possible.

Relevant: Dr. Wilkes, who is black, said he faced a lot of racism growing up in a mostly white area.

Irrelevant: As chair of the antiracism campaign, Dr. Trevor Wilkes, who is black, urged the school board to establish antiracism programs in all elementary and high schools.

Better: As chair of the antiracism campaign, Dr. Trevor Wilkes urged the school board to establish antiracism programs in all elementary and high schools.

- Avoid making generalizations about any racial or cultural group.

  Stereotyped: The Welsh are great singers.
  Better: The Welsh have a long tradition of singing.

- Use the word *ethnic* only as an adjective, never as a noun.

  Inappropriate: Many ethnics live in this area.
  Better: Many ethnic groups live in this area.

Sexist Language

Sexist language is language that degrades or unnecessarily excludes either women or men. It's best to avoid generalizing about males or females unless you are basing your claims on scientific fact.

- Whenever possible, replace words such as *fireman*, *policeman*, and *man-made* with non-sexist alternatives, such as *firefighter*, *police officer*, and *fabricated*.

- Avoid using the masculine pronouns *he*, *him*, or *his* to refer to both men and women. Instead, try one or more of the following methods:

  – Use the plural.

    Inappropriate: A good teacher can always command the respect of his students.
    Better: Good teachers can always command the respect of their students.

– Replace the pronoun with *the*, *a*, or *an*.

> **Inappropriate:** Whoever holds the winning ticket has not claimed his prize.
>
> **Better:** Whoever holds the winning ticket has not claimed the prize.

– Substitute *one* or *you*. Use *one* in more formal writing, and *you* in informal contexts.

> **Inappropriate:** A man never knows when his time will come.
>
> **Better:** One never knows when one's time will come. You never know when your time will come.

– Use *her* or *his*, *her* or *him*, or *she* or *he*. Note, however, that this method can start to sound a little awkward if used too often.

> **Inappropriate:** Each child will be given his own seat.
>
> **Better:** Each child will be given her or his own seat.

– Sometimes, the best way to avoid sexism is to change the wording of the sentence.

> **Inappropriate:** I've never met a nurse who was not rushed off her feet.
>
> **Better:** I've never met a nurse who was not in a great hurry.

Grammar

Contents

6

Parts of Speech

Every word in a sentence functions as one of the eight parts of speech. The four **main parts of speech** are

- nouns
- verbs
- adjectives
- adverbs

The four **other parts of speech** are

- pronouns
- prepositions
- conjunctions
- interjections

Just as actors take on different roles in different plays, so words can act as different parts of speech depending on the sentence. For example, in the first sentence below, the word *string* functions as a noun. In the second sentence, it acts as a verb. In the third, it is an adjective:

Noun: I found a piece of string in my soup.

Verb: String those beads to make a necklace.

Adjective: I use a string bag to carry my library books.

Noun

A noun is a word that refers to people, animals, things, places, qualities, or ideas. All of the highlighted words in the following sentence are nouns.

> When José was at the library in Guelph, his curiosity was aroused by an article that claimed chimpanzees could be cured of cancer by meditation.

The two main classes of nouns are common nouns and proper nouns.

Common nouns name general kinds of people, places, things, or ideas (e.g., *dog, person, movie, nation*). All nouns that are not proper nouns are common nouns.

Proper nouns name specific people, places, or things. Proper nouns are always capitalized (e.g., *Rover, Dominic, Frankenstein, Canada*).

In addition to classifying nouns as common or proper, some nouns are further classified as collective, compound, concrete, or abstract.

Collective nouns are singular in form but stand for a whole group (*class, herd, team, family*).

Concrete nouns name things that can be seen or touched (*house, leaf, mouse, river*).

Abstract nouns name ideas or qualities that cannot be sensed by sight or touch (*truth, justice, fear, freedom*).

Compound nouns are made up of two or more words that are treated as one. These nouns may be written as one word (*homework, sunlight*), as two separate words (*ice cream, hot dog*), or as a hyphenated word (*sister-in-law, runner-up*). Because the spelling of compound nouns tends to change over time—often evolving from two separate words, to a hyphenated word, and then to one word—you should check your dictionary for the most current spelling.

Grammar

Nouns, along with verbs, are the backbone of good writing, and it is generally better to use a single strong noun in place of a noun/adjective combination. A thesaurus is a good source of ideas. For example, here are some synonyms for *smell*:

the ∧~~warm, inviting smell~~ *aroma* of apple pie

the ∧~~horrible smell~~ *stench* of garbage

the ∧~~delicate, sweet smell~~ *fragrance* of cut flowers

the ∧~~characteristic smell~~ *odour* of a dog

the ∧~~lingering smell~~ *redolence* of perfume

Try Practice Exercise 1 on pages 127–128 and Practice Exercise 5 on page 129.

Verb

A verb is a word that tells what the subject is doing or experiencing. Most verbs express an action or a state of being. Verbs that express a state of being are sometimes called **linking verbs** because they link the subject to another word that describes the subject.

Action verbs: Sunil ran to school.

Dana thought about retiring.

Linking verb: Mariko seemed tired.

The verb *be* is the most common linking verb (for example, *am, is, are, was, were*), but others, such as *seem, appear, feel, smell,* and *look,* can be either linking or action verbs. To tell the difference, try replacing the verb with a form of *be.* If the meaning of the sentence remains the same, it is a linking verb.

John *felt* bad about throwing the pie.	["John *was* bad" does not have the same meaning, so *felt* is not a linking verb in this sentence.]
The blankets *felt* soft.	["The blankets *were* soft" has the same meaning, so *felt* is a linking verb in this sentence.]

Linking verbs are useful and necessary, but try to include as many strong action verbs as you can in your writing. Be especially careful not to begin your sentences with "There is" or "It is," except when necessary. The verb *be* has less impact than most action verbs. **See Verb Tense, p. 110; Subject–Verb Agreement, p. 118.**

Weak	Strong
There is a house on the hill.	A house looms on the hill.
There were two dogs in the playground.	Two dogs roamed the playground.
It was silent in the woods.	A silence enveloped the woods.

Try Practice Exercise 2 on page 128 and Practice Exercise 5 on page 129.

Adjective

An adjective is a word that describes a noun or a pronoun.

His soft, grey eyes made my heart melt.	[The adjectives *soft* and *grey* describe the noun *eyes*.]
She looked pale.	[The adjective *pale* describes the pronoun *She*.]

Avoid vague, overused adjectives such as *neat, good, nice, great, pretty* (as in *a pretty face*), *beautiful, fun, bad,* and *dumb.* Think about what you really want to say then find more accurate replacements in a thesaurus or dictionary.

Try Practice Exercise 3 on page 128 and Practice Exercise 5 on page 129.

Grammar

Adverb

An adverb can describe a verb, an adjective, another adverb, or a whole clause or sentence. Adverbs usually tell how, when, where, or in what manner.

That singer sings beautifully.　　[describes a verb]

I have an extremely tight schedule today.　　[describes an adjective]

I work too hard!　　[describes an adverb]

Strangely, the door was unlocked.　　[describes a whole clause]

Overused adverbs include *really, rather, very, somewhat, quite,* and *pretty* (as in *He was pretty upset*). Before you use one of these words, try the sentence without it to be sure it is necessary.

Weak: The movie was *really quite* entertaining, but it seemed *somewhat* long in places.

Strong: The movie was entertaining, but it seemed long in places.

Try Practice Exercise 3 on page 128 and Practice Exercise 5 on page 129.

Pronoun

A pronoun is a word that refers to someone or something without naming it directly. There are several types of pronouns.

Type of Pronoun	Examples		Sample Sentence
Personal	I he she we they you it mine hers theirs	me him her us them yours its his ours	Does Raphael know he has lost a button?

Type of Pronoun	Examples	Sample Sentence
Demonstrative	this that those these	This is the book I read last night.
Interrogative	who whom which what whose (when used in questions)	To whom did you wish to speak?
Reflexive	myself yourself himself	Don't go swimming by yourself.
Relative	who whom whose which that (when used to connect clauses)	The girl, whom I saw at the arena, lives on my street.
Indefinite	anyone somebody few all none each both neither some	I don't think anyone passed the test.

In addition, some pronouns (most of them personal pronouns) take different forms, or cases, depending on their function in a sentence. The three main forms of pronouns are the **subjective** (when the pronoun names the subject, or doer of the action), **objective** (when the pronoun tells who or what receives the action), and **possessive** (when the pronoun tells to whom or to what something belongs).

Subjective Pronouns	Objective Pronouns	Possessive Pronouns*
I	me	mine
you	you	yours
he	him	his
she	her	hers
it	it	its
we	us	ours
they	them	theirs
who	whom	whose

* Note that some people include the pronouns *my, your, her, our,* and *their* as possessive pronouns. Strictly speaking, however, these are possessive adjectives since they always modify a noun (*my house; your sister*).

In the sentence that follows, *they* performs the action ("gave"), *me* receives the action, and *theirs* tells who owns the sweatshirt in question.

<u>subjective</u>   objective   possessive

They gave me a sweatshirt just like theirs.

Often, a pronoun is used in place of a noun.

she

Hong was laughing because ~~Hong~~ found the joke funny

The word that a pronoun replaces is called its *antecedent*. When you use a pronoun to replace a noun, be sure that your reader can tell exactly what the antecedent is. You may also have to check that the form of pronoun you've chosen reflects the gender (e.g., *he* vs. *she*), number (e.g., *I* vs. *we*), and case (e.g., *he* vs. *him*) of its antecedent. You will find a lot more information on pronouns and antecedents in various parts of the Common Grammatical Errors section, beginning on page 117.

Try Practice Exercise 4 and Practice Exercise 5 on page 129.

Preposition

A preposition is a word that shows a relationship between a noun, called the *object of the preposition*, and another word that comes before it in the sentence. **See Object, p. 114.**

The house in the valley was swept away by the flood.
      prep.   object   prep.   object

Many words function as prepositions. Here are a few examples of some **common prepositions**:

above	for	since
at	from	to
before	in	through
behind	of	under
by	on	until
down	past	with

Be sure to avoid confusing the preposition *of* with the verb *have* in expressions such as *may have, could have, would have,* or *should have.* See Commonly Confused Words, p. 91.

> **Incorrect:** I could of been hurt!
> **Correct:**   I could have been hurt!

Try Practice Exercise 4 and Practice Exercise 5 on page 129.

Conjunction

A conjunction is a word that connects other words, phrases, clauses, ideas, or sentences. There are three types of conjunctions: co-ordinating, subordinating, and correlative. **Co-ordinating conjunctions** connect two similar words, phrases, or ideas. **Subordinating conjunctions** signal that one idea is less important than, or dependent on, another. **Correlative conjunctions** come in pairs, each introducing one of the two things being joined.

Type of Conjunction	Examples			Sample Sentence
co-ordinating	and but for	or so	nor yet	The dog barked, so I jumped.
subordinating	whenever because since	after if	before unless	Whenever the dog barked, I jumped.
correlative	both…and either…or	neither…nor not only…but also		Not only did the dog bark, but I also jumped.

Try Practice Exercise 5 on page 129.

Interjection

Interjections are short words or phrases that express strong emotion, such as shock, surprise, sorrow, excitement, or joy.

> Hey!   Oh!   Ouch!   Wow!   Yikes!

These types of words and expressions can be punctuated with a capital letter and an exclamation mark. For less intense emotions, you can include the interjection within a sentence, using a comma to set it apart from other words. Note the difference in tone in the following two sentences:

Hey, what are you doing?   Hey! What are you doing?

Try Practice Exercise 5 on page 129.

Verb Tense

The tense of a verb indicates whether the action took place in the past, present, or future.

Verb Tense	Example	Use
present	She tells.	for action that usually takes place in the present or to express general truths
past	She told.	for action completed in the past
future	She will tell.	for action that will occur in the future
present perfect	She has told.	for action begun in the past extending to the present
past perfect	She had told.	for action completed before another action in the past
future perfect	She will have told.	for action that will be completed by a specific time in the future
present progressive	She is telling.	for action that is ongoing in the present
past progressive	She was telling.	for action that was ongoing at a particular time in the past
future progressive	She will have been telling.	for action that will be ongoing at a specific time in the future

The present tense can also be used in a narrative to describe events in the past. However, it's important not to switch tenses in the middle of a piece of writing. If you have chosen to write in the present tense, use it consistently.

Confusing: Pedro walks up to the door. He had been waiting for this moment for the last two years. He reaches for the knocker and lets it fall. The door opens slowly, and there stood the biggest giant he ever saw.

Better: Pedro walked up to the door. He had been waiting for this moment for the last two years. He reached for the knocker and let it fall. The door opened slowly, and there stood the biggest giant he had ever seen.

OR

Pedro walks up to the door. He has been waiting for this moment for the last two years. He reaches for the knocker and lets it fall. The door opens slowly, and there stands the biggest giant he has ever seen.

Try Practice Exercise 6 on page 130.

Participle

A participle is a verb form that can be combined with a helping verb—such as *be* or *have*—to form tenses, but that cannot function as a verb on its own. The **present participle** of all verbs ends in *-ing* (*running, laughing, thinking, doing, being*). The **past participle** may end in *-ed*, *-en*, or *-t*, or various other ways (*called, given, bent, torn*). It is the form of the verb you would use after *have*.

Participles can also be used without a helping verb as adjectives in sentences.

> Laughing and talking, we ate burnt marshmallows and drank hot cocoa around the campfire.

When a participle is used as a noun, it is called a **gerund**.

> Running is a great sport.

Try Practice Exercise 7 on page 130.

Parts of a Sentence

A sentence is a group of words that expresses a complete thought. Every complete sentence has a subject and a predicate. These and other elements of sentences are described in this subsection.

Subject

The subject tells who or what the sentence is about.

> John ran.

The **complete subject** is all the words that describe who or what the sentence is about. The **simple subject** is the one most important noun or pronoun within the complete subject.

> simple subject
> A considerate member of the public reported the incident.
> complete subject

> simple subject
> Lean and hungry, the big grey wolf lunged at me.
> complete subject

Sometimes, two nouns joined by a conjunction form a compound subject.

> John and Tamia ran.

Although the subject is usually positioned before the verb, in some sentences, the order is reversed.

verb   subject   verb   subject
Down plunges the roller coaster!   Up comes my supper!

You need to be able to find the subject of your sentences in order to determine whether to use a singular or a plural verb. **See Subject–Verb Agreement, p. 118.**

Try Practice Exercise 8 and Practice Exercise 9 on page 131.

Predicate

The predicate of a sentence says what the subject did, was, felt, and so on. It always contains a verb.

John ran.

The **complete predicate** includes the verb and all the words that describe or complete the verb. The **simple predicate** is the verb itself, along with any helping verbs.

simple predicate
Marco had won the contest.
complete predicate

simple predicate
The police officer quickly caught the criminal.
complete predicate

Sometimes, a sentence has two or more verbs joined by a conjunction to form a **compound predicate**.

verb   conj.   verb
The ball hit the rim and bounced back.
compound predicate

Try Practice Exercise 8 and Practice Exercise 9 on page 131.

Object

The English language has three types of objects.

- A **direct object** is a noun or pronoun that answers the question *what?* or *who?* about the verb.

  He bought [what?] a kite.

- An **indirect object** answers the question *to what?*, *to whom?*, *for what?*, or *for whom?* about the verb.

  He bought [for whom?] me a kite.

- The **object of a preposition** is a noun or pronoun that comes at the end of a prepositional phrase. **See Phrase, p. 115.**

  He bought a kite <u>for me</u>.

It's easy to mistake the object of a preposition for the simple subject, and make the verb agree with it. But the object of a preposition is never the simple subject of a sentence.

A **group** *of my friends* **wants** to go camping.
simple subject   obj. of prep. **verb**

Try Practice Exercise 10 on page 131.

Subject Complement

A subject complement is a noun, pronoun, or adjective that comes after a linking verb. It tells something about the subject.

Mico is a painter.   It is he.   Your eyes look clear.

Try Practice Exercise 10 on page 131.

Clause

A clause is a group of words that has a subject and a verb. **Main clauses** (also known as *independent* or *principal clauses*) can stand on their own as full sentences, while **subordinate clauses** (also known as *dependent clauses*) need to be joined to a main clause. Subordinate clauses usually begin with a subordinating conjunction, such as *that, which, who, because, when, since.* **See Conjunction, p. 109; Sentence Types, p. 116.**

main clause   subordinate clause
This is the secret place that I like to visit.

main clause
Emily, who sometimes looks after our dog, is going to veterinary college.
subordinate clause

subordinate clause   main clause
When Riswan smiles, the whole room lights up.

Try Practice Exercise 11 on page 132.

Phrase

A phrase is a group of words that are used together in a sentence but that do not contain a subject and a predicate. Two types of phrases are prepositional phrases and participial phrases.

Prepositional phrases start with a preposition and end with a noun or pronoun. They can act as adjectives or adverbs in a sentence.

The dog crouched under the table.	[The prepositional phrase *under the table* functions as an adverb.]
I ordered a hamburger with fries.	[The prepositional phrase *with fries* functions as an adjective.]

Participial phrases begin with a present or past participle and can function as adjectives. **Compare Clause, p. 114.**

participial phrase   prepositional phrase
Broken beyond repair, the ship disappeared beneath the waves.

Try Practice Exercise 11 on page 132.

Sentence Types

Sentences come in three main types: simple, compound, and complex. Each of these three structures is described in this subsection.

Simple Sentence

A simple sentence has one main clause.

> Yukio's house has six bedrooms.

Try Practice Exercise 12 on page 132.

Compound Sentence

A compound sentence has two or more main clauses joined together by a semicolon or by a co-ordinating conjunction (*and, or, nor, for, but, so,* or *yet*).

> subject   verb   conj.   subject verb
> Yukio's house has six bedrooms, and the yard is huge.

Try Practice Exercise 12 on page 132.

Complex Sentence

A complex sentence has a main clause that can stand alone as a sentence, and one or more subordinate clauses.

> main clause
> Yukio's house, which he built himself, has six bedrooms.
> subordinate clause

Always put the most important thing you want to say in the main clause of a complex sentence.

Try Practice Exercise 12 on page 132.

Sentence Variety

Use a variety of sentence lengths and types when you write. When you revise, try mixing simple sentences with the occasional compound or complex sentence to create rhythm and make your writing flow.

Simple Sentences	vs.	Sentence Variety
I really enjoyed this book. It was so good. In fact, I could hardly put it down. The author included a lot of detail about pioneer life. The whole story seemed very real. Every character was believable. Each turn in the plot held me spellbound. I didn't expect to enjoy this book. However, I sure did!		I really enjoyed this book. It was so good I could hardly put it down. Because the author included a lot of detail about pioneer life, the story seemed very realistic. Every character was believable; every turn in the plot held me spellbound. I didn't expect to enjoy this book, but I sure did!

Try Practice Exercise 13 on page 133.

Common Grammatical Errors

You probably have an idea of the grammatical errors you tend to make, but it is a good idea to keep a record of these mistakes so that you can check for them when you proofread. Included here is a description of some of the most common pitfalls of English grammar. Check it whenever you are unsure of the conventions, and use it to help you proofread your own or other people's work.

Confusing Possessive and Plural Forms

Use possessive forms of nouns and pronouns to show ownership.

• To form the possessive of most singular nouns, add **'s**.

    Nick's idea   the cat's paw   Saskatoon's parks

- To form the possessive of plurals that end in -s, add an apostrophe.

  the students' project   the Livakos' pet   the cars' lights

- Plurals that do not end in -s form the possessive in the same way as singular nouns.

  children's games   people's pets   geese's flying patterns

- Proper nouns of two or more syllables that end in a **z** sound sometimes sound awkward when **'s** is added to form the possessive. For this reason, some writers prefer to omit the final **'s**.

  Laertes' death   Ramses' policies

A common error some writers make is using unnecessary apostrophes. Use these two questions to check whether an **'s** is needed:

#1 Can you reword the phrase using *of*? (e.g., Maria's coat = the coat of Maria).

#2 Can you substitute *is* or *has* for the **'s**? (e.g., Tanner's leaving = Tanner is leaving; Tanner's gone = Tanner has gone)

If the answer to both of these questions is "no," then an apostrophe is not needed.

no apostrophe

When he's had six colas, John's eye starts to twitch.
he has   the eye of John

Try Practice Exercise 14 on page 133.

Subject–Verb Agreement

A verb should always agree in number with its subject. Singular subjects take singular verbs, and plural subjects take plural verbs. When you are looking for the subject of a verb, remember the following tips:

- Prepositional phrases like *at school, under my desk, through the woods, with great sadness* never contain the subject of a sentence.

Be especially careful when the subject of the sentence is an indefinite pronoun like *one, all, each,* or *both.* These words are often followed by a prepositional phrase that separates the subject from the verb.

Incorrect: One of the cars were damaged.   [*cars* is not the subject]

Correct: One of the cars was damaged.   [the subject *One* needs a singular verb]

Incorrect: Both of the people in the van was safe.   [*van* is not the subject]

Correct: Both of the people in the van were safe.   [the subject *Both* is plural]

- The words *there* and *here* are not usually the subject of the verb even though they may appear immediately before the verb.

There are many reasons why I like you.   [*reasons* is the subject]

Here is my workbook.   [*workbook* is the subject]

- If a subject has two parts, joined by *or, not, either…or,* or *neither…nor,* make the verb agree with the part of the subject nearest to it.

                              plural   plural verb
Neither my brother nor my parents were at my recital.

                              singular singular verb
Neither my brother nor my sister was at my recital.

- Some subjects look plural when they are, in fact, singular.

The Diviners is a remarkable book.

The news comes on at six.

Five dollars is not enough to go to a movie.

Try Practice Exercise 15 on page 134.

Misplaced Modifier

Keep modifying words and phrases (for example, adjectives, adverbs, prepositional and participial phrases) as close as possible to the word they modify; otherwise, you may create a misplaced modifier.

                          modifier   word modified
Misplaced: Growling, my hat was being eaten by the dog.

Better: Growling, the dog was eating my hat.

                OR

                My hat was being eaten by a growling dog.

                word modified   modifier
Misplaced: She watched the moon rise from her chair.

Better: From her chair, she watched the moon rise.

Try Practice Exercise 16 on page 134.

Dangling Modifier

A dangling modifier occurs when the word being modified is implied but doesn't appear in the sentence. When you use a phrase to begin a sentence, make sure the word that follows it is the word it modifies.

                       phrase
Dangling: While jogging, the CD player broke.

                        word modified
Better: While jogging, I broke the CD player.

                       phrase
Dangling: Singing songs and cheering, the bus carried us home.

                           word modified
Better: Singing songs and cheering, we let the bus carry us home.

Try Practice Exercise 16 on page 134.

Double Negative

Using two negative words in the same sentence (such as *not* and *never*) creates an error called a *double negative*. Double negatives are often created in sentences where the word *not* is hidden in a contraction, such as *can't, won't,* or *don't*.

Double Negative: I can't barely look!
Corrected: I can barely look!

OR

I can't look!

Double Negative: There isn't scarcely enough to go around.
Corrected: There is scarcely enough to go around.

OR

There isn't enough to go around.

Try Practice Exercise 17 on page 135.

Unclear Pronoun Antecedent

It should be clear what word a pronoun replaces (its antecedent). Here are some examples of sentences with unclear antecedents:

Unclear: Lydia loves looking after Sandra because she is so good.
Clear: Lydia loves looking after Sandra because Sandra is so good.

OR

Lydia loves looking after Sandra because Lydia is so good.

Unclear: I completed the report, which pleased my teacher.
Clear: My teacher was pleased with the report I completed.

OR

My teacher was pleased because I completed the report.

Try Practice Exercise 18 on page 135.

Pronoun Case

Personal pronouns have three forms, or cases: the **subjective form** (*I, you, he, she, we, they*), the **objective form** (*me, you, him, her, us, them*), and the **possessive form** (*mine, yours, his, hers, ours, theirs*).

Although usually you will have no trouble choosing the right form, the following tips will help if you do run into difficulty:

- When the pronoun is joined to another noun or pronoun by *and, or,* or *nor,* pretend the other noun or pronoun is not there to see if the sentence sounds right.

Incorrect Case:	Neither Gloria nor me had ever met a lion face to face. [*me had met* is incorrect]
Correct:	Neither Gloria nor I had ever met a lion face to face. [*I had met* is correct]

Incorrect Case:	Ms. Singh sang songs to Saritsa and I. [*sang songs to I* is incorrect]
Correct:	Ms. Singh sang songs to Saritsa and me. [*sang songs to me* is correct]

- When the pronoun is part of a subject complement, *I* is technically correct even though in informal conversation you would likely say *It is me* rather than *It is I*. When you are writing formally, use the subjective case (*I, you, he, she, it, we, they*) for subject complements. **See Subject Complement, p. 114; Who/Whom, p. 126.**

  It was *she* who did all the work.

Pronouns and Gender

In the past, it was acceptable to use *he, him,* or *his* to refer to people in general. Expressions, sayings, and quotations from older sources often use *he, him,* or *his* in this way.

He who hesitates is lost.
He who pays the piper calls the tune.

Today, this usage is often considered unacceptable because it implies that women are not included. Although you may choose to rephrase sayings and expressions that have no known author (as shown below), it is best to leave direct quotations as is.

> Those who hesitate are lost.
> The one who pays the piper calls the tune.

In your own writing, be especially careful of using *he*, *him*, or *his* with indefinite pronouns, as in this example:

> Each of the players should bring his own water bottle.

This use of *his* to refer to the indefinite pronoun *each* is not acceptable—unless you know that all the players are male. In informal speech, people often solve the problem by using the plural form (*their own bottle*) even though the antecedent (*each*) is singular. In formal writing, however, you will need to find another way around the problem. **See Sexist Language, p. 98.**

Informal: Each of the players should bring *their* own water bottle.

Formal: Each of the players should bring *his or her* own water bottle.

OR

Each of the players should bring *a* water bottle.

OR

All players should bring *their* own water bottles.

Try Practice Exercise 19 on page 136.

Indefinite Pronouns

Indefinite pronouns can cause some problems with both subject–verb and pronoun–antecedent agreement. **See Subject–Verb Agreement, p. 118; Pronouns and Gender, p. 122.** When in doubt, use the following chart to decide whether a singular or plural verb is needed.

Use a Singular Verb with...	Use a Plural Verb with...	Use Either a Singular or a Plural Verb with... *
anybody/one/thing each either every everybody/one/thing little much neither nobody/ one/thing somebody/one/thing	both few many others several	all any more most none some

* The pronouns in the third column can take a singular or plural verb, depending on the meaning of the sentence.

> **Singular:** All of the cake is gone.
> **Plural:** All of the cookies are gone.

Try Practice Exercise 20 on page 136.

We and *Us* Before a Noun

Sometimes the pronouns *we* and *us* are used before a noun. In sentences like these, check that you are using the right form of the pronoun by reading the sentence without the noun. **See That/Which, below; Who/Whom, p. 126.**

Incorrect Case:	Us dog lovers love to talk about our pets.
	[*Us love to talk* is incorrect]
Correct:	We dog lovers love to talk about our pets.
	[*We love to talk* is correct]
Incorrect Case:	The actors gave we students a preview.
	[*The actors gave we a preview* is incorrect]
Correct:	The actors gave us students a preview.
	[*The actors gave us a preview* is correct]

Try Practice Exercise 19 on page 136.

That/Which

Informally, people often use *that* and *which* interchangeably. In formal writing, use *that* when the information in the clause that follows is a necessary part of the main idea in the sentence; use *which* when the information is not necessary to the sentence, and set off the clause with commas.

The coat that Mary bought is blue.	[*that Mary bought* tells us which specific coat we are talking about, so it is necessary to the main idea]
The coat, which Mary bought, is blue.	[*which Mary bought* tells us something else about the coat, but it is not part of the main idea; that is, that the coat is blue]

Grammar

Who/Whom

Who is a subjective form and *whom* is an objective form. **See Pronoun, p. 106.** If you are unsure about which form to use, try rewording part of the sentence using another subjective or objective pronoun, such as *she* or *her*. If *she* works, use *who*, but if *her* sounds right, use *whom*.

The boy *who starred in the play* won an award.

[*He starred in the play* is correct, so use *who*]

The boy *whom I saw in the play* won an award.

[*I saw him in the play* is correct, so use *whom*]

Try Practice Exercise 21 on page 137.

Run-on Sentence

A run-on sentence is formed when two sentences are run into one. To fix a run-on sentence, add the proper punctuation, or change the wording to make it a single sentence.

Run-on: The snow had melted it was spring at last.

Better: The snow had melted; it was spring at last.

OR

The snow had melted and it was spring at last.

OR

The snow had melted because it was spring at last.

Two sentences separated only by a comma is called a **comma splice**. Fix a comma splice the same way you would fix a run-on sentence.

Comma Splice: The doctor said I need rest, I am taking the week off.

Better: The doctor said I need rest; I am taking the week off.

OR

The doctor said I need rest, so I am taking the week off.

OR

Because the doctor said I need rest, I am taking the week off.

Try Practice Exercise 22 on page 137.

Sentence Fragment

A sentence fragment is a group of words that is set off as a sentence, but that lacks either a verb or a subject.

Fragment: We went to the game on Saturday. Josh and I. [*Josh and I* lacks a verb]
Revised: Josh and I went to the game on Saturday.

Fragment: Never did understand those engines. [*Never did understand those engines* lacks a subject]
Revised: I never did understand those engines.

Fragment: The water felt good. Cool and refreshing. [*Cool and refreshing* lacks both a subject and a verb]
Revised: The water felt cool and refreshing.

Sentence fragments are acceptable in informal writing, dialogue, and spoken English, but they are not appropriate in formal writing.

Try Practice Exercise 22 on page 137.

Practice Exercises

Practice Exercise 1: Noun

Identify each of the nouns in italic as abstract, collective, or proper. If the noun is also compound, note that as well.

1. *Beauty* is in the eye of the beholder.
2. My *concert band* is going on an exchange to England.
3. Did you enjoy reading *Obasan* by Joy Kogawa?
4. The *Parliament Buildings* once caught fire.
5. My sheepdog and I really value our *friendship*.

6. The *truth* is, I can't come to the movie because I'm sick.
7. I'm hoping that the *Blue Jays* will win the World Series this year.
8. A *herd* of sheep grazed peacefully on the hillside.
9. That *couple* has three children and they live on Joseph Street.
10. *Never* is a very long time.

Practice Exercise 2: Verb

Tell whether the verb in each of the following sentences is an action verb or a linking verb.

1. The sky seems clearer now.
2. The floor still looks muddy.
3. He didn't look both ways before crossing.
4. Logan smelled burning plastic in the kitchen.
5. His face appears flushed.
6. The chicken in the oven smells cooked.
7. Your voice sounds croaky.
8. Sound the alarm!
9. You feel sleepy because of the hot sun.
10. Sierra felt for the light switch in the dark.

Practice Exercise 3: Adjective, Adverb

Tell whether the words in italic are adjectives or adverbs. Then tell what word they modify.

1. We were *tired* and hungry after our journey.
2. I am *appalled* at your behaviour!
3. I had a *really* good time at your party.
4. I found a *real* spaceship in my backyard!
5. I was *never* good at public speaking.
6. I *very* nearly lost control of the car just then.
7. *Yesterday*, I dreamed I saw a giant lobster.
8. I had *two* cream puffs for lunch.
9. You look *ill*.
10. The *small* bedroom is painted midnight blue.

Practice Exercise 4: Pronoun, Preposition

Identify the words in italic as either a pronoun (PRON) or a preposition (PREP).

1. One cubic centimetre *of* brain contains ten billion bits of information and *it* processes five thousand bits a second.
2. *Those* are my memories of *her*.
3. When *I* was a little girl, I heard many stories *about* my family.
4. *Most* of the postcards said *we* should come down and see the city.
5. If *anyone* phoned *while* she was practising, we were supposed to say she was unavailable.
6. Do *you* need *somebody* to go to the store?
7. Feeling his way *along* the ledge, he did not dare look *toward* the ground.
8. Kate asked *herself who* would do such a thing.
9. The cougar jumped *out* of sight *between* two cedars.
10. Then *everyone* looked *beyond* the town at a column of smoke.

Practice Exercise 5: Parts of Speech

Identify the part of speech of each of the italicized words in the sentences that follow.

1. I *love* to take my *hamster* windsurfing.
2. *Mackenzie and* I got stuck at the top of the ferris wheel for an hour.
3. *Hey,* what do you mean by *that*?
4. Tread *softly* as *you* walk past the baby's room.
5. The carpet is worn *to threads* at the top of the stairs.
6. I *skinned* my knee *badly* when I fell off my bike.
7. A fine *layer* of moss *now* covered the rock.
8. I wanted to make the flowers smell *better, so* I sprayed them with perfume.
9. The wailing siren made *it* difficult to talk *quietly*.
10. Kamal has *two* absences *on* his report card.

> Some Practice Exercises cover more than one topic (note the exercise heading). You may need to refer to more than one topic within the Section before completing an exercise.

Grammar

Practice Exercise 6: Verb Tense

Rewrite the following passage, correcting any unnecessary changes in tense.

> It was the scariest few moments of my life. We are flying back to Toronto from St. John's (where we had been on holiday for two weeks) when there is suddenly a big commotion. All the attendants are running around looking flustered. They told us all to put on our seatbelts, and then the captain comes on the intercom to report that the landing gear wasn't working properly! He says we have to make an emergency landing in Bangor, Maine. We were told to assume the emergency landing position, with our hands on the back of the seat in front. I'm shaking like a leaf, and so is everyone else, but no one screamed or started crying. We were all very, very quiet for the entire descent, just hanging on, breathing hard, and trying not to panic.
>
> Well, we made it. It was a rough landing, but no one was hurt. I never thought I would be so happy to see the airport at Bangor, Maine!

Practice Exercise 7: Participle

Find a participle in each of the following sentences and tell whether it is acting as part of a verb (V) or as an adjective (A).

1. I was running so fast that my shoes were on fire!
2. That's why I didn't bring my running shoes for gym today.
3. My nicely browned piece of toast just fell in the sink.
4. Crying softly, the little boy ran through the busy market to find his mother.
5. Ashley had broken her pelvis in a fall from a horse.
6. To make a perfect cup of tea, always use boiling water.
7. I am trying to build a rocket out of these blocks of wood.
8. Offended by my remark, she left the room in a huff.
9. The ruined house is at the end of the street.
10. Her claim to fame was her laughing eyes.

Practice Exercise 8: Subject, Predicate

Identify the complete subject and complete predicate in each of the following sentences.

1. The grizzly bear is a beautiful animal.
2. Mahdi and William became hopelessly lost in the fun house.
3. Up from his hole popped a little brown groundhog.
4. That book of matches could have started a fire.
5. The great big scary mountain in the distance turned out to be just a molehill.
6. Holding on to the bar for dear life and watching as the ground zoomed up to meet me, I swore never to ride another roller coaster.
7. Superman, that gallant superhero with the red cape, had come to Earth from a dying planet.
8. Without luck on our side, the score would have been a lot closer.
9. A flock of birds squawked and fluttered over our heads.
10. A pounding of hooves was heard in the distance.

Practice Exercise 9: Subject, Predicate

Now go back and identify the simple subject and simple predicate in each of the sentences in Practice Exercise 8.

Practice Exercise 10: Object, Subject Complement

Identify the direct object in each of these sentences. If the sentence has a subject complement instead of a direct object, write SC next to it.

1. The water of the hot spring felt soothing to my aching joints.
2. My brother spent ten dollars on that book.
3. Carla broke my bike!
4. Rivka seems perfectly happy to stay with you.
5. My uncle gave me some good advice.
6. I wrote a poem just for you.
7. Arnold was once a police officer.
8. I felt the grass tickling my feet.
9. I ate some chicken for supper.
10. Hold the end of this stick for me.

Grammar

Practice Exercise 11: Clause, Phrase

Tell whether each of the groups of words in italic is a clause or a phrase. Mark MC for main clauses, SC for subordinate clauses, PREP for prepositional phrases, and PART for participial phrases.

1. *In the early morning*, we left to go fishing.
2. I sat *in the front of the boat*.
3. *When they saw us coming*, the fish apparently left in a hurry.
4. We sat there for hours, *waiting for a nibble*.
5. At one point, we passed another boat *piled high with fish*.
6. *We wondered* why we couldn't seem to catch anything.
7. *After a while* it didn't seem to matter much.
8. *The waves were lapping* against the side of the boat.
9. Before we knew it, *lulled by the waves*, we were both fast asleep.
10. So we did catch something, although it wasn't *what we had expected*: a nap.

Practice Exercise 12: Simple Sentence, Compound Sentence, Complex Sentence

Tell whether each of the following sentences is simple, compound, or complex.

1. The tool that I was using to fix the air conditioner fell inside the machine.
2. Every day, at exactly 5:00 a.m., the birds in my garden start to create a huge commotion.
3. I'd love to go, but I can't.
4. When it rains, it pours.
5. It was a blistering hot day, so I turned on the hose full blast for the kids.
6. In a small dark corner of the attic, I found a locked chest without a key.
7. You are going to tidy your room whether you want to or not!
8. He could not see it or feel it, but he knew it was there.
9. Once there was a boy with eyes as blue as the sky and a girl with eyes as green as the sea, and they lived together with their parents in a land as old as the hills.
10. My bike, before I outgrew it, was my most prized possession.

Practice Exercise 13: Sentence Variety

Rewrite the following passage, joining some of the simple sentences into compound or complex sentences.

> I was six. I had a pet snail for a few days. I called it Harry. I made a house for it out of an old cardboard box. I taped plastic wrap across the top. I put half an avocado, some leaves from the garden, and a couple of my toys in the box. The snail climbed up the side. It couldn't escape. I had done too good a job with the masking tape. A few days later, my mother wanted me to put it back in the garden. I didn't want to let it go. I was afraid. I would never find it again. Then I had a great idea. I got out my paint box. I chose a bright red. I painted the snail's shell. I knew I would always be able to find it.

Practice Exercise 14: Confusing Possessive and Plural Forms

Rewrite the following passage, correcting any errors in the use of apostrophes and plurals.

> I have two family's. Theres the family I have with my mom, my stepdad, and my two half sister's. Then there's the one I have on alternate week's with my dad, his wife, and her two boy's from a previous marriage. To make thing's even more confusing, sometimes the two boy's stay at their fathers' house.
>
> Coincidentally, both my mothers' are teachers. What's more, Dad's a librarian, while my stepfather runs a childrens' bookstore. But the parallels don't stop there. The girls names are Taylor and Mack (for Mackenzie), while the boys' names are Tyler and Max! Sometime's it drive's me crazy, trying to tell my two household's apart, but the truth is, I wouldn't give up either of them for anything.

Practice Exercise 15: Subject–Verb Agreement

Correct any errors in subject–verb agreement in the following sentences. If the sentence is correct, mark C.

1. Mathematics is a very logical science.
2. A poll taken by the Tories seem to indicate that the election will be close.
3. There's too many players on the field.
4. Neither James nor Nerusan knows what happened.
5. Both of the wiper blades on the car needs changing.
6. Everyone from Grades 6, 7, 8, and 9 are welcome to attend the performance.
7. News of world events travel fast over the Internet.
8. Here are some refreshments for your friends.
9. One of my two dogs are sick.
10. Animatronics are a cross between animation and electronics, and is used to create special effects for movies.

Practice Exercise 16: Misplaced Modifier, Dangling Modifier

Rewrite each of the following sentences to correct any misplaced or dangling modifiers.

1. Speaking slowly, the class could hear every word I said during my oral presentation.
2. I was still in bed when the alarm clock rang in my pyjamas.
3. Unable to walk because of her arthritis, the wheelchair helped my grandmother become mobile again.
4. Yesterday we found a box containing an old piece of paper, which was made of wood.
5. Alone, the house felt much creepier than before.
6. Each of the tropical fish species has a name in this aquarium that is decidedly odd, such as pink kisser, marble angel, and rummy nose.
7. We tiptoed past as the baby slept peacefully, hardly daring to breathe in case she woke.
8. Swimming upstream, the eggs are laid at the spawning ground by the salmon before it dies.
9. While waiting for real coins to arrive by ship from Europe, playing cards were often used by the government of New France to pay its workers.
10. Wings spread, I watched as the majestic hawk soared above me.

Practice Exercise 17: Double Negative

Rewrite the following sentences in two different ways, eliminating the double negative each time.

1. I can't barely wait until Saturday.
2. My friend Jake can't wait neither.
3. I have hardly no interest in cars.
4. We hadn't seen nobody since Friday.
5. They weren't going nowhere fast!
6. Since they paved over the wetland, those ducks don't have nowhere to live.
7. I don't have nothing to do.
8. Maya wouldn't eat none of the cake.
9. I don't get no respect.
10. Samir hasn't never been late before.

Practice Exercise 18: Unclear Pronoun Antecedent

The following sentences have unclear pronoun antecedents. Rewrite the sentences in two different ways, making the antecedent clear each time. You may have to add or change words in the sentence.

1. The dog in that yard which is very big once growled at me.
2. My parents met your parents when they were on their honeymoon.
3. Veronica and Maria went to her sister's house.
4. Although he gave me a present on my birthday, it wasn't very nice.
5. That man owns a picture of an old house, which I want to buy.
6. Ahmed drove Terry to his home town.
7. Carmen visited Margit whenever she was well enough.
8. When the van hit the car, it was badly damaged.
9. When Philip and Nathan play chess, he always wins.
10. People with small children should make sure they get enough sleep.

Practice Exercise 19: Pronouns and Gender, *We* and *Us* Before a Noun

Correct any errors in the use of pronouns in these sentences. If the sentence is correct, mark C.

1. Us counsellors have just as much fun as you campers do.
2. Zoltan and me planted trees near our camp.
3. It wasn't me who ate the butter tarts.
4. Anyone who didn't bring their water bottle may buy a drink.
5. Any advertiser who thinks simple marketing ploys will fool we kids is crazy!
6. It was her who said that us girls were being too noisy.
7. Her and the boys went skating last Saturday.
8. Some of the skaters were showing off their tricks.
9. Everyone who wants a part in the play has to write their name on the list.
10. No one thinks that we Panthers stand a chance against that other team.

Practice Exercise 20: Indefinite Pronouns

Choose the correct verb or pronoun form given in parentheses to agree with the indefinite pronoun in each sentence.

1. Neither of the boys (is/are) going to play soccer this year.
2. If anybody (recognize/recognizes) any of (his or her/their) belongings in the Lost and Found box, (he or she/they) should take them home before the end of school.
3. None of the gold bars (was/were) ever found.
4. Most of those who tried to find the treasure (was/were) never seen again.
5. Some of the desserts from the party (is/are) left over.
6. One of the planes (is/are) going off course.
7. Are both of the trees losing (its/their) leaves?
8. Most of the film (was/were) over by the time we arrived.
9. Every one of you girls (has/have) (her/their) own way of doing things.
10. Nobody on either of the teams (want/wants) to forfeit the game.

Practice Exercise 21: Who/Whom

Choose the subjective (who) or objective (whom) form of the pronoun to complete these sentences.

1. (Who/Whom) shall I say is calling?
2. The women (who/whom) fought for their right to vote were called suffragettes.
3. I'll introduce you to my family, (who/whom) you've never met.
4. I've never known a student (who/whom) is as smart as Ethan.
5. (Who/Whom) do you wish you could be?
6. The painters, (who/whom) we hired to work on our new house, did an excellent job.
7. You can invite (whoever/whomever) you want to your party.
8. I wonder (who/whom) you saw peering through the window of the store.
9. To (who/whom) should I address this e-mail?
10. There was a bully in my school (who/whom) used to make my life miserable.

Practice Exercise 22: Run-on Sentence, Sentence Fragment

Rewrite the following passage, correcting run-on sentences and fragments.

> In the 1930s, the world economy collapsed and countries were plunged into a Great Depression, it lasted until the Second World War in 1939. Some countries were hit especially hard. Canada for one, since it depended so much on trade with other countries. Many people lost all their money and many others found themselves without a job as businesses failed, the number of unemployed people was staggering. One-third of all Canadians who were old enough to work, to be precise.
>
> At first, there was no government employment insurance or other assistance programs to help these people, in fact, many of them suffered from malnutrition. Especially single men, who often had to go to work in government-run relief camps. The work in the camps was very hard. Planting trees, building roads and buildings, and clearing brush, for example, all for twenty cents a day, plus room and board. Some chose not to enter the camps, instead, they preferred to travel the country as hobos, picking up work or begging for food where they could.

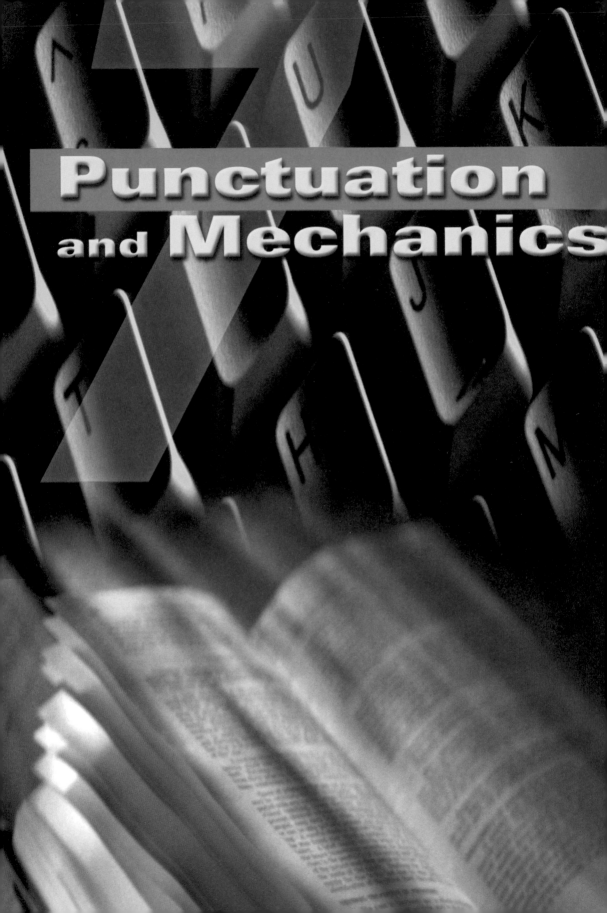

Punctuation
and Mechanics

Contents

7

Punctuation Marks

For better or for worse, punctuation can have a dramatic effect on your writing. Marks of punctuation are the signposts that tell your readers when to pause, when to stop, when to draw connections between ideas. Without them, your words run together in an endless stream; used improperly, punctuation can change, or obscure, the meaning of your words. For this reason, it is worth taking some extra time when you proofread to make sure that you have used end marks, commas, quotation marks, and other punctuation correctly.

Apostrophe [']

Apostrophes can be used

- to show possession (*Jane's boat*)

- to indicate a contraction (*don't; can't; she's*)

- to replace missing letters in speech (*How 'bout you?*)

- to replace missing numbers in a date (*the Class of '99*)

- to show the plural of letters or symbols (*There are three a's in Saskatchewan and two 0's in 2003.*)

See Confusing Possessive and Plural Forms, p. 117.

Try Practice Exercise 1 on page 156 and Practice Exercise 2 on page 157.

Colon [:]

A colon warns you that something is to follow. Use colons in the following situations:

- to introduce a list

  Colours have specific meanings in different cultures: in North America, for example, red often stands for danger, black suggests mourning, and green implies nature.

- to express time

    8:45; 20:00

- to separate the volume and page numbers of a magazine

    Food Lover's Digest, 4:17–19

- after the salutation in a business letter

    Dear Ms. Rosen:

Try Practice Exercise 3 on page 157 and Practice Exercise 7 on page 159.

Comma [,]

A comma indicates a slight pause in a sentence. Most modern writers use as few commas as possible without confusing the reader. Use a comma

- between compound sentences (if the sentences are short, the comma may be omitted)

    Rula thought hard, but no solutions came to mind.

- when you say someone's name to address them

    David, please take the garbage out.

- with words, phrases, or clauses that interrupt a sentence

    We will, nevertheless, do our best to win.

    The whole family cheered when, for the first time, the baby hiccupped.

    Marcel, who has thick hair, can never get his bathing cap on.

- with introductory words, phrases, or clauses

    Naturally, George was pleased.

    In the end, I stayed home and read.

    When we had finished eating, we took the boat out for a spin.

- between items in a series

    Geoff, Willem, and Aviva work together at the factory.

Some writers omit the comma just before the *and* in a series. This is acceptable as long as it is done consistently and the sentences are still clear.

- to set off *which* clauses

| The roller skates, which are black, fit me perfectly. | [*which are black* is not essential to the main idea] |

    BUT

| The roller skates that are black fit me perfectly. | [*that are black* identifies which roller skates are being discussed, so it is part of the main idea] |

See That/Which, p. 125.

See That/Which, p. 125.

- in addresses when they are part of a sentence (note that there is no comma before the postal code)

    Please send an information kit to Serge Laflamme, 334 Grosvenor Avenue, Montréal, Québec H3H 3C7.

    BUT

    Serge Laflamme
    334 Grosvenor Avenue
    Montréal, Québec H3H 3C7

- in some forms of dates

    January 14, 2007   BUT   14 January 2007

- between a city and a province or country

    Fredericton, New Brunswick   London, England

- in salutations of personal letters

    Dear Sam,

- to set off degrees and titles

    Peter Lavigne, Ph.D   Lorraine Mishinski, M.P.

Try Practice Exercise 4 and Practice Exercise 5 on page 158, and Practice Exercise 7 on page 159.

Dash [-- or —]

A dash marks a strong break in a sentence.

> It wasn't until Friday—or it may have been Saturday—that I discovered my wallet was missing.

> Did you ever see the film—but no, it was made before you were born.

> Three students—Ruby, Aamina, and Michael—were named as finalists.

> Jack works hard—when he has to.

Dashes are useful for emphasis, but too many can make your writing disjointed and difficult to read. Consider using other punctuation, such as commas or parentheses, instead.

Try Practice Exercise 6 on page 158.

Ellipsis Points [...]

To show that words have been cut from within a quotation, use ellipsis points, a series of three periods (...). If you cut words from the end of a quoted sentence, add a fourth dot to serve as the period (....). Put any added words or explanations that are not part of the original quotation in square brackets.

Original quotation:

Without commercialism, you cannot organize an Olympic Games. It is impossible. We need money for the Olympic Games, but at the same time, money must not run the Games. We need commercialism but this commercialism must be controlled.   *Juan Antonio Samaranch, President, International Olympic Committee*

Shortened version:

According to IOC President Juan Antonio Samaranch, "Without commercialism, you cannot organize an Olympic Games....[The Games] need money...but at the same time...commercialism must be controlled."

Also use ellipsis points to show that a sentence trails off or is left unfinished.

KIM: Well, I...um...I just don't know....

Try Practice Exercise 8 on page 159.

Exclamation Mark [!]

An exclamation mark gives emphasis, and expresses surprise, delight, or alarm.

Hey!   How sweet!   Watch out!

When used sparingly, exclamation marks can be helpful, but too many can weaken their effect. Rather than rely on punctuation marks, trust your choice of words to express emotions.

Weak: The room was a mess! Tables were overturned! The drawers had been pulled out! I understood immediately! The apartment had been robbed!!!!

Better: The room was a mess. Tables were overturned. The drawers had been pulled out. I understood immediately—the apartment had been robbed!

Try Practice Exercise 9 on page 161.

Hyphen [-]

Hyphens are used in the following ways:

- to spell compound numbers from 21 to 99 (*twenty-one*; *seventy-five*)

- to spell out times of day in formal writing (*the five-fifteen bus*)

- to spell out fractions (*one-half of the pie*)

- in some numerical expressions (*a thirteen-year-old boy; a twenty-dollar bill*)

- in many expressions formed with prefixes, especially those beginning with *all-*, *ex-*, *half-*, *pro-*, and *self-*, or when not having a hyphen might be confusing

all-round	co-operate	de-ice	ex-boyfriend
half-baked	pro-Canadian	re-elect	self-centred

Note that because there are many exceptions to these rules, it is best to check your dictionary for guidance.

- when a two-word modifier precedes a noun, unless the first word ends in *-ly*

    rosy-fingered dawn   BUT   carefully woven cloth

- in some compound nouns

    merry-go-round   jack-rabbit   voice-over

  Note, however, that because many compound nouns are written as one word (e.g., *handbook*), or as two words with or without a hyphen (e.g., *hand-stand; hand brake*) it's best to check your dictionary for the right form.

- to divide a word between syllables at the end of a line (*dis-satisfied; dissat-isfied; dissatis-fied*)

  Sometimes word breaks are necessary, but try to avoid them whenever possible. In particular, do not break a word at the end of a page, and avoid leaving only one or two letters of a word on a line by themselves.

> **Avoid:** Please don't take these comments on your performance too personal-ly.

> **Better:** Please don't take these comments on your performance too personally.

Note that proper nouns (nouns that begin with a capital letter) and words of only one syllable should never be broken.

Try Practice Exercise 10 and Practice Exercise 11 on page 161.

Parentheses [( )]

Use parentheses to set off comments or asides in a sentence.

> They lived happily ever after (and so did the dog).

When necessary, you can use punctuation marks inside the parentheses, even in the middle of a sentence.

> All of us except Shannon (Shannon is always optimistic!) were sure it was going to rain.

You can place whole sentences in parentheses. If the sentence stands alone, punctuate it as you would a regular sentence.

> The French colony of Upper Volta, now called Burkina Faso, gained its independence in 1960. (Burkina Faso means "Land of honest men.")

Try Practice Exercise 7 on page 159.

Period [.]

Use a period

- to mark the end of a sentence (*The sky is blue.*)

- after initials and abbreviations (*J. J. Cale; Mr.; St.*)

Note that there is a space after each period in initials.

See Quotation Marks, p. 148.

Try Practice Exercise 9 on page 161 and Practice Exercise 12 on page 162.

Question Mark [?]

A question mark indicates a direct question. Don't use a question mark when the question is indirect.

Direct Questions:	Where is the remote?
	Do you know where the remote is?
Indirect Questions:	Sasha asked where the remote was.
	I wonder where the remote is.

See Quotation Marks, p. 148.

Try Practice Exercise 9 on page 161 and Practice Exercise 12 on page 162.

Quotation Marks [" "]

The three main uses for quotation marks are as follows: for titles, for direct quotations (including dialogue within a narrative), and for words that define or describe.

- **Titles:** Use quotation marks for works that are usually contained within a longer work, collection, or anthology.

Short Stories	Magazine Articles	News Articles
"Survival Ship"	"Canada's Comedians"	"Election called for June 2"

Short Poems	Songs	Episodes in a Television Series
"The Bull Calf"	"Suzanne"	"Artichoke Pie" is tonight's *Black Harbour* episode.

- **Quotations:** Use quotation marks to show that the words inside are a direct quotation. Very long quotations (over 100 words, or over three lines of your writing) that are indented from the body of the text don't need quotation marks.

  Use a comma between the speaker's tag (for example, *Camilla asked*) and the quotation unless the quotation ends with a question mark or an exclamation mark and the speaker's tag follows.

  > Camilla asked, "Where is the notebook you borrowed?"

  OR

  > "Where," asked Camilla, "is the notebook you borrowed?"

  BUT

  > "Where is the notebook you borrowed?" asked Camilla.

  A period or comma at the end of a quotation goes inside the quotation marks.

  > "The trouble is," he muttered, "I can't get the time machine to work."

A semicolon at the end of a quotation goes outside the quotation marks.

> Sarah announced, "I don't want any more cookies, thank you"; then she sank back down in the bed and slept until morning.

A question mark or exclamation mark goes inside the quotation marks if it relates to the quoted material, and outside if it applies to the whole sentence.

> Theo called out, "Where are you going?"
>
> BUT
>
> I'm tired of hearing you say, "I'll clean it up tomorrow"!

Use single quotation marks for a quotation within a quotation.

> Horace wailed, "Did you say, 'They are lost'?"

- **Definitions and Descriptions:** You can also use quotation marks in place of italics or underlining to indicate a word that is being defined or explained.

> The term "downsizing" is a euphemism that usually means firing a lot of employees.

Avoid the temptation of putting slang or colloquial words in quotation marks to make them more acceptable. If you feel they are inappropriate, don't use them; otherwise, use them without quotation marks.

> **Imprecise:** That boy over there has a real "attitude."
> **Precise:**   That boy over there has a bad attitude.

Try Practice Exercise 8 on pages 159–160 and Practice Exercise 13 on page 162–163.

Semicolon [;]

Use a semicolon to separate two related sentences.

I love watching television after school; it relaxes me.

Semicolons are also used to separate items in a list when one or more of the items contains a comma.

Walter has lived in Tokyo, Japan; London, England; and Estevan, Saskatchewan.

See Quotation Marks, p. 148.

Try Practice Exercise 3 on page 157.

Capitalization

Capitalize the following:

- the first word in a sentence or a quotation

    Here is how one book defines a computer virus: "A dangerous program that can delete or scramble data or shut down your computer."

- all proper nouns (words that name a particular person, place, or thing)

    A Swiss man, George de Mestral, invented Velcro after examining the burrs that had stuck to his coat while he walked his dog.

- the main words in a title

    "O Canada"   Mathematics 201   *Romeo and Juliet*

- titles and family relationships, when used as part of a person's name

  I saw Dad reading. BUT I saw my dad reading.

  I went to Doctor Namis BUT I went to the doctor
  for a check-up. for a check-up.

- days of the week, months, and holidays

  Tuesday September Ramadan

- businesses and organizations, political parties, and religions

  Roots the United Nations the Liberal Party Judaism

- historical events, eras, and documents

  the Seven Years' War the Great Depression the BNA Act

- celestial bodies

  Jupiter Earth the North Star

- all the letters in acronyms (words that are made up of the first letters of a title)

  NATO (North Atlantic Treaty Organization)

  UNICEF (United Nations International Children's Educational Fund)

Try Practice Exercise 14 on page 163.

Italics and Underlining

Use *italics* when working on a computer (or <u>underlining</u> when writing by hand) to identify a whole work.

Books	Films	Newspapers	Magazines
Blood Red Ochre	*Attack of the Killer Tomatoes*	*The Vancouver Sun*	*TG Magazine*

Plays	Long Poems	Works of Art	TV Programs/Series
A Midsummer Night's Dream	*The Owl and the Pussycat*	*Birth of Venus*	*Hockey Night in Canada*

Italics and underlining can also be used in the following ways:

- to emphasize certain words

  To avoid charges of bias, the committee listened to arguments both for *and* against the proposal.

- to show a word that is being defined or referred to as a word

  My dictionary defines *fatuous* as "stupid but self-satisfied."

- to indicate a foreign word or phrase

  The Soviet policy of *glasnost*, or openness, ended the Cold War.

See Quotation Marks, p. 148.

Try Practice Exercise 13 on pages 162–163.

Abbreviation

An abbreviation is a shortened form of a word or phrase. There is a trend away from using periods in many abbreviations, especially names of companies or organizations (e.g., the UN, the CBC).

While abbreviations are useful in lists, tables, footnotes, and technical documents, only some are acceptable in formal writing or in school assignments. Check the charts that follow to find out which abbreviations you can use.

- Abbreviations that can be used in both formal and informal writing include the following:

Abbreviation	Examples	Use
Titles before a name	Mr., Mrs., Ms., Dr., Rev.	Mr. Alfred Turner Dr. Hannah Elfstrom
Degrees and titles after a name	Ph.D., B.A., C.A., M.D.	Harry Shaftoe, C.A.
St. for Saint in place names	St. Laurent St. John's	St. John's, Newfoundland BUT Saint John, New Brunswick
Time expressions	a.m. (or AM) p.m. (or PM) B.C., A.D., B.C.E., C.E.	7:00 p.m. A.D. 456
Company or organization names (use the full name with the abbreviation in parentheses the first time; then use the abbreviation only)	C.B.C. or CBC U.N. or UN R.C.M.P. or RCMP C.A.W. or CAW (Note that there is a trend away from the use of periods in abbreviated company names.)	The Canadian Broadcasting Corporation (CBC) is funded by the Government of Canada. People who work for the CBC are government employees.

- Here are some abbreviations that are useful in bibliographies and footnotes:

Abbreviation	Meaning
ed.	editor; edition
et al.	and others
ibid.	the same as before
pp.	pages
rev.	revised
trans.	translator
vol.	volume

- Abbreviations such as those in the chart that follows can be used in scientific writing, or in any writing in which you use a lot of measurements and numbers. With numbers written out as words, though, always spell out the abbreviation (e.g., either *6 L* or *six litres*, not *six L*).

Abbreviation	Meaning
°C	degrees Celsius
cm	centimetre
ha	hectare
in.	inch
kg	kilogram
km	kilometre
L	litre
lb.	pound
m	metre
mL	millilitre
oz.	ounce
t	tonne
yd.	yard

- When taking notes or writing informally, you might find these abbreviations useful:

Abbreviation	Meaning
cf.	compare
co.	company
e.g. *	for example
etc.	and others; and so on
i.e. *	that is
inc.	incorporated
N.B.	note
no.	number

* This abbreviation should always be followed by a comma.

- When addressing letters and envelopes, you can use the following short forms. Note that the abbreviations for provinces and compass directions are written without periods.

Abbreviation	Meaning
Apt.	Apartment
Ave.	Avenue
Blvd.	Boulevard
Dr.	Drive
N, S, E, W	North, South, East, West
NE, NW	Northeast, Northwest
P.O.	Post Office
Rd.	Road
SE, SW	Southeast, Southwest
St.	Street (or Saint)
AB	Alberta
BC	British Columbia

Punctuation and Mechanics

Abbreviation	Meaning
LB	Labrador
MB	Manitoba
NB	New Brunswick
NF	Newfoundland
NS	Nova Scotia
NT	Northwest Territories and Nunavut
ON	Ontario
PE	Prince Edward Island
QC	Québec
SK	Saskatchewan
YT	Yukon

Try Practice Exercise 15 and Practice Exercise 16 on page 164.

Practice Exercises

Practice Exercise 1: Apostrophe [']

Rewrite the following sentences, adding apostrophes where they are needed.

1. My computers spell checker automatically noticed that I put three ss in the word *misspell* instead of two.
2. Its not easy to find anyone in Western Canada who was alive in the 1930s who wasnt affected by the Great Depression.
3. "Im goin down to the beach tsee if the wavesre still high," said Alonso.
4. Yuris collection of comic books isnt for sale.
5. "Yall know that Is the best darn poker player aroun," drawled the cowboy.

Practice Exercise 2: Apostrophe [']

Choose the correct word in parentheses to complete each of the following sentences.

1. I think (your/you're) coming down with a cold.
2. (Theirs/There's) a nasty cold going around our school.
3. My friends tell me (its/it's) wreaking havoc in (theirs/there's) as well.
4. (Theirs/There's) hardly anyone (whose/who's) managed to avoid (its/it's) clutches.
5. (Your/You're) best bet is to rest in bed and drink a lot of water.

Practice Exercise 3: Colon [:], Semicolon [;]

Rewrite the following letter, replacing some of the existing punctuation with a colon or a semicolon where necessary.

> Dear Ms. Vautour,
>
> Congratulations! You are the winner of our Tour of Canada's Capitals contest. The motto you suggested for our ice cream was chosen as the winning entry at our corporate headquarters on May 6, from now on, all our ice cream and ice milk products will bear your inspiring words, "Nice and sweet; an ice-cold treat."
>
> Your trip will begin at 9 15 on the morning of July 1st, Canada Day. A limousine will arrive to carry you and your guest to the airport, there, a private jet will be waiting to take you on the first leg of your journey.
>
> Included in your tour are the following stops, Victoria, B.C., Whitehorse, Yukon, Yellowknife, Northwest Territories, Edmonton, Alberta, Regina, Saskatchewan, Winnipeg, Manitoba, Toronto, Ontario, Québec City, Québec, Fredericton, New Brunswick, Halifax, Nova Scotia, Charlottetown, P.E.I., St. John's, Newfoundland, and finally, Canada's newest capital, Iqaluit, in the Territory of Nunavut.
>
> A complete itinerary will be forwarded to you within the next two weeks. Enjoy your trip!
>
> Regards,
>
> Samuel Mboto
> Marketing Manager
> Tasty Treat Company

Practice Exercise 4: Comma [,]

Write the convention that explains why the comma(s) in each sentence is (are) necessary.

1. There was hardly the whisper of a breeze blowing that night, yet the flag was standing straight out from the flagpole.
2. Ivan, could you please pass the salt?
3. My doctor, who never seems to get sick, told me to take vitamin C every day.
4. Coincidentally, we ended up at the same restaurant as the Markovics that night.
5. Lily, Patrick, and Darshan went fishing yesterday.

Practice Exercise 5: Comma [,]

Add commas where they are needed in the following sentences.

1. When the roof of the tent started to sag from the rain we all got a little nervous.
2. Thinking fast I opened my umbrella.
3. Unfortunately I hit Jason in the eye.
4. Jason startled by the jab threw his hands out and hit the tent's roof which started the leak.
5. My friend there is nothing as depressing as a waterlogged tent at five in the morning.

Practice Exercise 6: Dash [-- or —]

Insert the missing dashes in the following sentences.

1. That woman my great-grandmother was the first woman telegrapher on the CPR.
2. We have agreed to set aside our differences for now.
3. I'm e-mailing you the document in a format that I hope you can read a Wordperfect file.
4. One day I'm told it won't be too long from now we will all have computer chips implanted in our brains.
5. There is only one place that I can really call my own my room.

Practice Exercise 7: Colon [:], Comma [,], Parentheses [( )]

Now look back at the sentences you corrected in Practice Exercise 6. Find a way to eliminate the dashes, either by rewording the sentence or by substituting commas, colons, or parentheses.

Practice Exercise 8: Ellipsis Points [...], Quotation Marks [" "]

Read the following quotations; then, check through the abbreviated versions (marked **Extract**), making any necessary changes to the punctuation.

1. **Original Source:** I want to go on making a contribution to life. I'm going to college and maybe study communication. I hope I can continue to influence people. I like to be noticed for *who* I am, not *what* I am. But I don't wish I was able-bodied anymore. I used to. I can experience some regular things, but then I can do things other people can't. I can speed down the school hallway really fast. Being this way gives me a unique view of the world.

    from "Character in Action: Ryan Schroer: Carrying the Torch"
    by Barbara A. Lewis

    Extract: Ryan Schroer, a student with cerebral palsy, has big plans for his future: I'm going to college and maybe study communication. I hope I can continue to influence people. But I don't wish I was able-bodied anymore. Being this way gives me a unique view of the world.

2. **Original Source:** But I don't think dreams are meant to work out. They are based on ignorance after all, on how we respond to the way the world looks before we know what it is like, or really what we are like. It is the act of dreaming that is important, the daily process of putting together a future that a girl can move toward with confidence and desire.

    from "Horse Love" by Jane Smiley

    Extract: Jane Smiley writes, I don't think dreams are meant to work out. It is the act of dreaming that is important, the daily process of putting together a future that we can move toward with confidence and desire.

3. **Original Source:** *Street Cents* is based all across Canada. We have our main production centre in Halifax, Nova Scotia. That's where the studio segments are shot and where the show is put together. We also have producers working in several different Canadian cities. They put together the "field" segments, which are the stories that come from outside the studio.

from Street Cents Web site

Extract: According to the *Street Cents* Web site, *Street Cents* has its main production centre in Halifax, Nova Scotia where the studio segments are shot and where the show is put together. They also have producers working in several different Canadian cities who put together the stories that come from outside the studio.

4. **Original Source:** In the dead of night, we tiptoed into the Trip Cabin. As my colleagues blissfully snored, we glued all their shoes to the floor. We then filled them full of horse manure, and covered the door handle with shaving foam. We spread more manure on the porch; after this, we climbed up onto the roof and jumped up and down. When we judged that the occupants of the cabin were fully awake and about to come after us, we skinned down off the roof, ran back to our own cabins and jumped into bed. Meanwhile, the Trippers were trying to put on their shoes, failing, grappling with the slithery door handle, and running out onto the manure-covered porch in their bare feet.

from "Capering" by Margaret Atwood

Extract: Margaret Atwood recalls a practical joke she played while working as a camp counsellor in Ontario: In the dead of night, Beryl Fox and I tiptoed into the Trip Cabin that housed the male trip counsellors. As my colleagues blissfully snored, we glued all their shoes to the floor. We then filled them full of horse manure, and covered the door handle with shaving foam. We spread more manure on the porch; after this, we climbed up onto the roof and jumped up and down. Then we ran back to our own cabins. Meanwhile, the counsellors were trying to put on their shoes, failing, grappling with the slithery door handle, and running out onto the manure-covered porch in their bare feet.

Practice Exercise 9: Exclamation Mark [!], Period [.], Question Mark [?]

Add periods, question marks, and one exclamation mark to the spaces provided in the following passage.

> I wonder why computers always crash when you are in the middle of an important assignment__ Just today, I was putting the finishing touches on my English paper when the thing checked out on me__ And why are the troubleshooting sections in manuals always so useless__ I mean, is anyone really stupid enough to need the warning "Be sure that the computer is plugged in and all the cords are properly connected"__ It's crazy… It's useless… It's… Oops__ Could you please excuse me while I plug in my keyboard__

Practice Exercise 10: Hyphen [-]

Add hyphens where necessary in the following sentences.

1. Two thirds of the students in my class did well on the exam.
2. I ran into my ex coach downtown, with his ten year old daughter.
3. At half time, only ninety eight people were left in the stands.
4. I drew a three dimensional plan that is self explanatory.
5. It would take an exceptionally hard hearted person to resist the smile on that big eyed baby!

Practice Exercise 11: Hyphen [-]

Indicate at least one place where each of the following words could be broken at the end of a line. If the word cannot be broken, write NO BREAK.

1. simplicity
2. Toronto
3. screamed
4. contented
5. professional

Practice Exercise 12: Period [.], Question Mark [?]

Add a period to indirect questions and a question mark to direct questions.

1. a) Would you mind holding the door for me__
   b) I wonder if you would mind holding the door for me__
   c) I asked if you would mind holding the door for me__

2. a) Brendan asked if the pizza was ready__
   b) Is the pizza ready yet__
   c) I was wondering if the pizza was ready__

3. a) What's the name of that girl, I wonder__
   b) Do you know the name of that girl__
   c) I wonder if you know the name of that girl__

4. a) Her name should be in the register, shouldn't it__
   b) Check the register, would you__
   c) She inquired if she could check the register__

5. a) I wonder, is that the North Star up there__
   b) I wonder if that is the North Star__
   c) That could be the North Star, couldn't it__

Practice Exercise 13: Quotation Marks [" "], Italics and Underlining

Rewrite the following sentences, adding quotation marks or underlining as needed.

1. Please turn to the third chapter, titled Make Your Own Rocket.
2. We saw a really interesting film in class yesterday called The Life of a Snail.
3. When we were in Italy, we went to see Michelangelo's famous sculpture, David.
4. Anyone who has read Shakespeare's play Romeo and Juliet will recognize the plot and characters in the film West Side Story.
5. I'm reading a creepy short story called Night of the Mutant Eggs from a collection of short stories titled Tales of the Unexpected.
6. I found an article titled Training Your Hamster to Juggle in a magazine called Hamster News, and it got me all excited.

7. I could just see the newspaper headlines: Juggling Hamster Wows Crowds at World's Fair!
8. They might even put us on Oprah!
9. Stompin' Tom might write a song about my hamster, called Joe the Juggler or The Hamster Song.
10. Unfortunately, Joe won't co-operate; all he wants to do is watch Hammy the Hamster reruns on the TV.

Practice Exercise 14: Capitalization

Add capitals to the following sentences.

1. there are over 250 000 muslims, or followers of the islamic religion, in canada.
2. our family doctor, who is from pakistan, was telling me about some of his beliefs.
3. for one thing, dr muhammad says practising muslims must pray five times a day and during the season of fasting, known as ramadan, they cannot eat or drink from dawn until dusk.
4. a census taken just four years after confederation showed only thirteen people claiming to be muslim.
5. in 1931, during the great depression, this number had risen to 645.
6. it was not until after world war two that large numbers of muslims entered canada, so that by 1971 there were about 33 000 muslims recorded in the country.
7. but it has been in recent times that the real explosion of muslim immigrants to canada has taken place, according to *the canadian encyclopedia*.
8. the encyclopedia says: "over 60% of muslims in canada are foreign-born, having immigrated during the last twenty years."
9. anyway, dad says I've learned so much about islam from talking to our doctor that I should use the information as part of my project for social studies 301.
10. this year, ramadan will take place in november, which is just when my project is due.

Punctuation and Mechanics

Practice Exercise 15: Abbreviation

List all the abbreviations in the following sentences and then circle which abbreviations are appropriate for formal writing.

1. Mr. Jones—i.e., the new supervisor—is moving here from St. John's, NF.
2. I work for Cantech Inc., a company that supplies automobile parts to some of the major car makers, i.e., General Motors (GM) and Ford.
3. I will look forward to meeting you at 3:00 p.m. at 275 Albert St.
4. The successful candidate should have a degree in a relevant field (e.g., a B.Sc. in computers or robotics).
5. According to the Swampville Trail Association, or STA, if you intend to hike the entire length of the fifteen-km trail, you should be sure to bring adequate supplies (i.e., food, extra clothing, etc.).

Practice Exercise 16: Abbreviation

Replace at least one word or phrase in each sentence with an abbreviation.

1. John Doe, editor, *Poems by Anonymous Poets*, volume 3, revised edition (Erewhon: Nonesuch Press, 1999), pages 16–18.
2. Apartment for rent. Apply 240 Westwood Road, number 2B.
3. Please note: The hole should measure 78 inches, or 2 metres exactly.
4. The United Way is a charitable organization that raises money for all kinds of good causes (such as the Kids Help Phone, Big Brothers, and others).
5. At about three o'clock this afternoon, a spokesperson for the International Olympic Committee will be holding a news conference and a reporter for the Canadian Broadcasting Corporation will be there.

Section 6: Grammar

Practice Exercise 1: Noun *Page 127*
1. abstract
2. collective, compound
3. proper
4. proper, compound
5. abstract
6. abstract
7. proper, compound
8. collective
9. collective
10. abstract

Practice Exercise 2: Verb *Page 128*
1. seems (linking)
2. looks (linking)
3. didn't (action)
4. smelled (action)
5. appears (linking)
6. smells (linking)
7. sounds (linking)
8. Sound (action)
9. feel (linking)
10. felt (action)

Practice Exercise 3: Adjective, Adverb *Page 128*
1. adjective modifying *we*
2. adjective modifying *I*
3. adverb modifying *good*
4. adjective modifying *spaceship*
5. adverb modifying *good*
6. adverb modifying *nearly*
7. adverb modifying *dreamed*
8. adjective modifying *cream puffs*
9. adjective modifying *you*
10. adjective modifying *bedroom*

Practice Exercise 4: Pronoun, Preposition *Page 129*
1. of (PREP)   it (PRON)
2. Those (PRON)   her (PRON)
3. I (PRON)   about (PREP)
4. Most (PRON)   we (PRON)
5. anyone (PRON)   while (PREP)
6. you (PRON)   somebody (PRON)
7. along (PREP)   toward (PREP)
8. herself (PRON)   who (PRON)
9. out (PREP)   between (PREP)
10. everyone (PRON)   beyond (PREP)

Practice Exercise 5: Parts of Speech *Page 129*
1. verb, noun
2. noun, conjunction
3. interjection, pronoun
4. adverb, pronoun
5. preposition, noun
6. verb, adverb
7. noun, adverb
8. adjective, conjunction
9. pronoun, adverb
10. adjective, preposition

Practice Exercise 6: Verb Tense *Page 130*

It was the scariest few moments of my life. We **were** flying back to Toronto from St. John's (where we had been on holiday for two weeks) when there **was** suddenly a big commotion. All the attendants **were** running around looking flustered. They told us all to put on our seatbelts, and then the captain **came** on the intercom to report that the landing gear wasn't working properly! He **said** we **had** to make an emergency landing in Bangor, Maine. We were told to assume the emergency landing position, with our hands on the back of the seat in front. I **was** shaking like a leaf, and so **was** everyone else, but no one screamed or started crying. We were all very, very quiet for the entire descent, just hanging on, breathing hard, and trying not to panic.

Well, we made it. It was a rough landing, but no one was hurt. I never thought I would be so happy to see the airport at Bangor, Maine!

Practice Exercise 7: Participle
Page 130
1. running (V)
2. running (A)
3. browned (A)
4. Crying (A)
5. broken (V)
6. boiling (A)
7. trying (V)
8. Offended (A)
9. ruined (A)
10. laughing (A)

Practice Exercise 8: Subject, Predicate *Page 131*

complete subject/*complete predicate*

1. **The grizzly bear** *is a beautiful animal.*
2. **Mahdi and William** *became hopelessly lost in the fun house.*
3. *Up from his hole popped* **a little brown groundhog.**
4. **That book of matches** *could have started a fire.*
5. **The great big scary mountain in the distance** *turned out to be just a molehill.*
6. **Holding on to the bar for dear life and watching as the ground zoomed up to meet me, I** *swore never to ride another roller coaster.*
7. **Superman, that gallant superhero with the red cape,** *had come to Earth from a dying planet.*
8. **Without luck on our side, the score** *would have been a lot closer.*
9. **A flock of birds** *squawked and fluttered over our heads.*
10. **A pounding of hooves** *was heard in the distance.*

Practice Exercise 9: Subject, Predicate *Page 131*

	Simple Subject	Simple Predicate
1.	bear	is
2.	Mahdi and William	became
3.	groundhog	popped
4.	book	could have started
5.	mountain	turned (out)
6.	I	swore
7.	Superman	had come
8.	score	would have been
9.	flock	squawked and fluttered
10.	pounding	was heard

Practice Exercise 10: Object, Subject Complement *Page 131*
1. The water of the hot spring felt **soothing** to my aching joints. (SC)
2. My brother spent **ten dollars** on that book.
3. Carla broke **my bike**!
4. Rivka seems **perfectly happy** to stay with you. (SC)
5. My uncle gave me **some good advice**.
6. I wrote **a poem** just for you.
7. Arnold was once **a police officer**. (SC)
8. I felt **the grass** tickling my feet.
9. I ate **some chicken** for supper.
10. Hold **the end** of this stick for me.

Practice Exercise 11: Clause, Phrase *Page 132*
1. PREP
2. PREP
3. SC
4. PART
5. PART
6. MC
7. PREP
8. MC
9. PART
10. SC

Practice Exercise 12: Simple Sentence, Compound Sentence, Complex Sentence *Page 132*

1. complex
2. simple
3. compound
4. complex
5. compound
6. simple
7. complex
8. compound
9. compound
10. complex

Practice Exercise 13: Sentence Variety *Page 133*

Answers will vary. A suggested revision follows.

When I was six, I had a pet snail for a few days. I called it Harry. I made a house for it out of an old cardboard box and taped plastic wrap across the top. I put half an avocado, some leaves from the garden, and a couple of my toys in the box. Although the snail climbed up the side, it couldn't escape because I had done too good a job with the masking tape.

A few days later, when my mother wanted me to put it back in the garden, I didn't want to let it go. I was afraid that I would never find it again. Then, I had a great idea. I got out my paint box, chose a bright red, and painted the snail's shell so I would always be able to find it.

Practice Exercise 14: Confusing Possessive and Plural Forms
Page 133

I have two **families**. **There's** the family I have with my mom, my stepdad, and my two half **sisters**. Then there's the one I have on alternate **weeks** with my dad, his wife, and her two **boys** from a previous marriage. To make **things** even more confusing, sometimes the two **boys** stay at their **father's** house.

Coincidentally, both my **mothers** are teachers. What's more, Dad's a librarian, while my stepfather runs a **children's** bookstore. But the parallels don't stop there.

The **girls'** names are Taylor and Mack (for Mackenzie), while the boys' names are Tyler and Max! **Sometimes** it **drives** me crazy, trying to tell my two **households** apart, but the truth is, I wouldn't give up either of them for anything.

Practice Exercise 15: Subject–Verb Agreement *Page 134*

1. C
2. A poll taken by the Tories **seems** to indicate that the election will be close.
3. **There are** too many players on the field.
4. C
5. Both of the wiper blades on the car **need** changing.
6. Everyone from Grades 6, 7, 8, and 9 **is** welcome to attend the performance.
7. News of world events **travels** fast over the Internet.
8. C
9. One of my two dogs **is** sick.
10. Animatronics **is** a cross between animation and electronics, and is used to create special effects for movies.

Practice Exercise 16: Misplaced Modifier, Dangling Modifier *Page 134*

Answers will vary slightly. Some suggested revisions follow.

1. Because I spoke slowly during my oral presentation, the class could hear every word I said.
2. When the alarm clock rang, I was still in bed in my pyjamas.
3. The wheelchair helped my grandmother, who was unable to walk because of her arthritis, become mobile again.
4. Yesterday we found a wooden box containing an old piece of paper.
5. Being alone in the house made it feel much creepier than before.

6. Each of the tropical fish species in this aquarium has a name that is decidedly odd, such as pink kisser, marble angel, and rummy nose.

7. As the baby slept peacefully, we tiptoed past, hardly daring to breathe in case she woke.

8. The salmon swims upstream and lays its eggs at the spawning ground before it dies.

9. While waiting for real coins to arrive by ship from Europe, the government of New France often used playing cards to pay its workers.

10. I watched as the majestic hawk, wings spread, soared above me.

Practice Exercise 17: Double Negative *Page 135*

1. I can barely wait until Saturday. / I can't wait until Saturday.

2. My friend Jake can't wait either. / Neither can my friend Jake wait.

3. I have no interest in cars. / I have hardly any interest in cars.

4. We hadn't seen anybody since Friday. / We had seen nobody since Friday.

5. They were going nowhere fast! / They weren't going anywhere fast!

6. Since they paved over the wetland, those ducks have nowhere to live. / Since they paved over the wetland, those ducks don't have anywhere to live.

7. I don't have anything to do. / I have nothing to do.

8. Maya wouldn't eat any of the cake. / Maya would eat none of the cake.

9. I don't get any respect. / I get no respect.

10. Samir has never been late before. / Samir hasn't ever been late before.

Practice Exercise 18: Unclear Pronoun Antecedent *Page 135*

Answers will vary slightly. Some suggested revisions follow.

1. The very big dog in that yard once growled at me. / The dog in that very big yard once growled at me.

2. My parents met your parents when my parents were on their honeymoon. / My parents met your parents when your parents were on their honeymoon.

3. Veronica and Maria went to Veronica's sister's house. / Veronica and Maria went to Maria's sister's house.

4. Although he gave me a present on my birthday, my birthday wasn't very nice. / Although he gave me a present on my birthday, the present wasn't very nice.

5. That man owns a picture I want to buy of an old house. / That man owns a picture of an old house I want to buy.

6. Ahmed drove Terry to Ahmed's home town. / Ahmed drove Terry to Terry's home town.

7. Whenever Carmen was well enough, she visited Margit. / Carmen visited Margit whenever Margit was well enough.

8. When the van hit the car, the car was badly damaged. / The van was badly damaged when it hit the car.

9. When Philip and Nathan play chess, Philip always wins. / Nathan always wins when he and Philip play chess.

10. People with small children should make sure their children get enough sleep. / People should make sure they get enough sleep, especially if they have small children.

Practice Exercise 19: Pronouns and Gender, *We* and *Us* Before a Noun *Page 136*

1. **We** counsellors have just as much fun as you campers do.

2. Zoltan and **I** planted trees near our camp.

3. It wasn't **I** who ate the butter tarts.

4. Anyone who didn't bring **a** water bottle may buy a drink.

5. Any advertiser who thinks simple marketing ploys will fool **us** kids is crazy!

6. It was **she** who said that **we** girls were being too noisy.

7. **She** and the boys went skating last Saturday.

8. C

9. Everyone who wants a part in the play has to write **his or her** name on the list.

10. C

Practice Exercise 20: Indefinite Pronouns *Page 136*

1. Neither of the boys **is** going to play soccer this year.

2. If anybody **recognizes** any of **his or her** belongings in the Lost and Found box, **he or she** should take them home before the end of school.

3. None of the gold bars **were** ever found.

4. Most of those who tried to find the treasure **were** never seen again.

5. Some of the desserts from the party **are** left over.

6. One of the planes **is** going off course.

7. Are both of the trees losing **their** leaves?

8. Most of the film **was** over by the time we arrived.

9. Every one of you girls **has her** own way of doing things.

10. Nobody on either of the teams **wants** to forfeit the game.

Practice Exercise 21: Who/Whom *Page 137*

1. **Who** shall I say is calling?

2. The women **who** fought for their right to vote were called suffragettes.

3. I'll introduce you to my family, **whom** you've never met.

4. I've never known a student **who** is as smart as Ethan.

5. **Whom** do you wish you could be?

6. The painters, **whom** we hired to work on our new house, did an excellent job.

7. You can invite **whomever** you want to your party.

8. I wonder **whom** you saw peering through the window of the store.

9. To **whom** should I address this e-mail?

10. There was a bully in my school **who** used to make my life miserable.

Practice Exercise 22: Run-on Sentence, Sentence Fragment *Page 137*

Answers will vary. A suggested revision follows.

In the 1930s, the world economy collapsed and countries were plunged into a Great Depression (that) lasted until the Second World War in 1939. Some countries were hit especially hard. Canada (was) one (of these,) since it depended so much on trade with other countries. Many people lost all their money and many others found themselves without a job as businesses failed. (The) number of unemployed people was staggering: one-third of all Canadians who were old enough to work, to be precise.

At first, there was no government employment insurance or other assistance programs to help these people. (In) fact, many of them suffered from malnutrition— (e)specially single men, who often had to go to work in government-run relief camps. The work in the camps was very hard. (It included) (p)lanting trees, building roads and buildings, and clearing brush, for example, all for twenty cents a day, plus room and board. Some chose not to enter the camps. (Instead,) they preferred to travel the country as hobos, picking up work or begging for food where they could.

Section 7: Punctuation and Mechanics

Practice Exercise 1:
Apostrophe ['] *Page 156*

1. My computer's spell checker automatically noticed that I put three s's in the word misspell instead of two.

2. It's not easy to find anyone in Western Canada who was alive in the 1930s who wasn't affected by the Great Depression.

3. "I'm goin' down to the beach t' see if the waves're still high," said Alonso.

4. Yuri's collection of comic books isn't for sale.

5. "Y'all know that I's the best darn poker player aroun'," drawled the cowboy.

Practice Exercise 2:
Apostrophe ['] *Page 157*

1. I think **you're** coming down with a cold.

2. **There's** a nasty cold going around our school.

3. My friends tell me **it's** wreaking havoc in **theirs** as well.

4. **There's** hardly anyone **who's** managed to avoid **its** clutches.

5. **Your** best bet is to rest in bed and drink a lot of water.

Practice Exercise 3: Colon [:],
Semicolon [;] *Page 157*

Dear Ms. Vautour:

Congratulations! You are the winner of our Tour of Canada's Capitals contest. The motto you suggested for our ice cream was chosen as the winning entry at our corporate headquarters on May 6; from now on, all our ice cream and ice milk products will bear your inspiring words: "Nice and sweet; an ice-cold treat."

Your trip will begin at 9:15 on the morning of July 1st, Canada Day. A limousine will arrive to carry you and your guest to the airport; there, a private jet will be waiting to take you on the first leg of your journey.

Included in your tour are the following stops: Victoria, B.C.; Whitehorse, Yukon; Yellowknife, Northwest Territories; Edmonton, Alberta; Regina, Saskatchewan; Winnipeg, Manitoba; Toronto, Ontario; Québec City, Québec; Fredericton, New Brunswick; Halifax, Nova Scotia; Charlottetown, P.E.I.; St. John's, Newfoundland; and finally, Canada's newest capital, Iqaluit, in the Territory of Nunavut.

A complete itinerary will be forwarded to you within the next two weeks. Enjoy your trip!

Regards,

Samuel Mboto
Marketing Manager
Tasty Treat Company

Practice Exercise 4: Comma [,]
Page 158

1. to separate main clauses in a compound sentence

2. after the name of someone being addressed in a sentence

3. to set off words or phrases that interrupt a sentence

4. after an introductory word

5. between items in a series

Practice Exercise 5: Comma [,]
Page 158

1. When the roof of the tent started to sag from the rain, we all got a little nervous.

2. Thinking fast, I opened my umbrella.

3. Unfortunately, I hit Jason in the eye.

4. Jason, startled by the jab, threw his hands out and hit the tent's roof, which started the leak.

5. My friend, there is nothing as depressing as a waterlogged tent at five in the morning.

Practice Exercise 6: Dash [--] or [—] *Page 158*

1. That woman—my great-grandmother—was the first woman telegrapher on the CPR.

2. We have agreed to set aside our differences—for now.

3. I'm e-mailing you the document in a format that I hope you can read—a Wordperfect file.

4. One day—I'm told it won't be too long from now—we will all have computer chips implanted in our brains.

5. There is only one place that I can really call my own—my room.

Practice Exercise 7: Colon [:], Comma [,], Parentheses [( )] *Page 159*

Answers will vary slightly. Some suggested revisions follow.

1. That woman, my great-grandmother, was the first woman telegrapher on the CPR.

2. We have agreed to set aside our differences (for now).

3. I'm e-mailing you the document in a format that I hope you can read: a Wordperfect file.

4. One day (I'm told it won't be too long from now) we will all have computer chips implanted in our brains.

5. There is only one place that I can really call my own: my room.

Practice Exercise 8: Ellipsis Points [...], Quotation Marks [" "] *Page 159*

1. Ryan Schroer, a student with cerebral palsy, has big plans for his future: "I'm going to college and maybe study communication. I hope I can continue to influence people.... But I don't wish I was able-bodied anymore.... Being this way gives me a unique view of the world."

2. Jane Smiley writes, "...don't think dreams are meant to work out....It is the act of dreaming that is important, the daily process of putting together a future that [we] can move toward with confidence and desire."

3. According to the *Street Cents* Web site, "*Street Cents* ...[has its] main production centre in Halifax, Nova Scotia...where the studio segments are shot and where the show is put together [They] also have producers working in several different Canadian cities [who] put together...the stories that come from outside the studio."

4. Margaret Atwood recalls a practical joke she played while working as a camp counsellor in Ontario: "In the dead of night, [Beryl Fox and I] tiptoed into the Trip Cabin [that housed the male trip counsellors]. As my colleagues blissfully snored, we glued all their shoes to the floor. We then filled them full of horse manure, and covered the door handle with shaving foam. We spread more manure on the porch; after this, we climbed up onto the roof and jumped up and down....[Then we] back to our own cabins....Meanwhile, the [counsellors] were trying to put on their shoes, failing, grappling with the slithery door handle, and running out onto the manure-covered porch in their bare feet."

Practice Exercise 9: Exclamation Mark [!], Period [.], Question Mark [?] *Page 161*

I wonder why computers always crash when you are in the middle of an important assignment. Just today, I was putting the finishing touches on my English paper when the thing checked out on me. And why are the troubleshooting sections in manuals always so useless? I mean, is anyone really stupid enough to need the warning "Be sure that the computer is plugged in and all the cords are properly connected"? It's crazy... It's useless... It's... Oops! Could you please excuse me while I plug in my keyboard?

Practice Exercise 10: Hyphen [-] *Page 161*

1. Two-thirds of the students in my class did well on the exam.

2. I ran into my ex-coach downtown, with his ten-year-old daughter.

3. At half-time, only ninety-eight people were left in the stands.

4. I drew a three-dimensional plan that is self-explanatory.

5. It would take an exceptionally hard-hearted person to resist the smile on that big-eyed baby!

Practice Exercise 11: Hyphen [-]
Page 161

Note: Syllable breaks that are marked • are suitable word breaks.
A dash (–) indicates a syllable that should not be broken.

1. sim•pli•ci–ty

2. NO BREAK

3. NO BREAK

4. con•tent–ed

5. pro•fes•sion–al

Practice Exercise 12: Period [.], Question Mark [?] *Page 162*

1. a) Would you mind holding the door for me?
   b) I wonder if you would mind holding the door for me.
   c) I asked if you would mind holding the door for me.

2. a) Brendan asked if the pizza was ready.
   b) Is the pizza ready yet?
   c) I was wondering if the pizza was ready.

3. a) What's the name of that girl, I wonder.
   b) Do you know the name of that girl?
   c) I wonder if you know the name of that girl.

4. a) Her name should be in the register, shouldn't it?
   b) Check the register, would you?
   c) She inquired if she could check the register.

5. a) I wonder, is that the North Star up there?
   b) I wonder if that is the North Star.
   c) That could be the North Star, couldn't it?

Practice Exercise 13: Quotation Marks [" "], Italics and Underlining *Page 162*

1. Please turn to the third chapter, titled "Make Your Own Rocket."

2. We saw a really interesting film in class yesterday called The Life of a Snail.

3. When we were in Italy, we went to see Michelangelo's famous sculpture, David.

4. Anyone who has read Shakespeare's play Romeo and Juliet will recognize the plot and characters in the film West Side Story.

5. I'm reading a creepy short story called "Night of the Mutant Eggs" from a collection of short stories titled Tales of the Unexpected.

6. I found an article entitled "Training Your Hamster to Juggle" in a magazine called Hamster News, and it got me all excited.

7. I could just see the newspaper headlines: "Juggling Hamster Wows Crowds at World's Fair!"

8. They might even put us on Oprah!

9. Stompin' Tom might write a song about my hamster, called "Joe the Juggler" or "The Hamster Song."

10. Unfortunately, Joe won't co-operate; all he wants to do is watch Hammy the Hamster reruns on the TV.

Practice Exercise 14: Capitalization *Page 163*

1. There are over 250 000 Muslims, or followers of the Islamic religion, in Canada.

2. Our family doctor, who is from Pakistan, was telling me about some of his beliefs.

3. For one thing, Dr. Muhammad says practising Muslims must pray five times a day and during the season of fasting, known as Ramadan, they cannot eat or drink from dawn until dusk.

4. A census taken just four years after Confederation showed only thirteen people claiming to be Muslim.

5. In 1931, during the Great Depression, this number had risen to 645.

6. It was not until after (World) (War) (Two) that large numbers of Muslims entered (Canada), so that by 1971 there were about 33 000 (Muslims) recorded in the country.

7. But it has been in recent times that the real explosion of (Muslim) immigrants to (Canada) has taken place, according to (The) (Canadian) (Encyclopedia).

8. (The) encyclopedia says: "(Over) 60% of (Muslims) in (Canada) are foreign-born, having immigrated during the last twenty years."

9. (Anyway,) (Dad) says I've learned so much about (Islam) from talking to our doctor that I should use the information as part of my project for (Social) (Studies) 301.

10. (This) year, (Ramadan) will take place in (November), which is just when my project is due.

Practice Exercise 15: Abbreviation
Page 164

Abbreviations that may be used in formal writing are circled.

1. (Mr.)	i.e.	(St.)	NF
2. (Inc)	i.e.	(GM)	
3. (p.m)	St.		
4. e.g.	B.Sc.		
5. (STA)	km	i.e.	etc.

Practice Exercise 16: Abbreviation
Page 164

All possibilities are circled.

1. John Doe, (ed), *Poems by Anonymous Poets*, (vol) 3, (rev. ed) (Erewhon: Nonesuch Press, 1999), (pp.) 16–18.

2. (Apt.) for rent. Apply 240 Westwood (Rd), (no.) 2B.

3. (N.B.) The hole should measure 78 (in.) or 2 (m) exactly.

4. The United Way is a charitable organization that raises money for all kinds of good causes, (e.g.) the Kids Help Phone, Big Brothers, (et al.).

5. At about (3:00 p.m.) a spokesperson for the (IOC) will be holding a news conference and a reporter for the (CBC) I will be there.

Index

Acknowledgments

Every reasonable effort has been made to trace ownership of copyrighted material. Information that would enable the publisher to correct any reference in future editions would be appreciated.

11 Excerpt from "The Jade Peony" by Wayson Choy. ©Wayson Choy. / **11** Excerpt from "The Transformations of Cindy R." by Anne Mazer from *Stay True: Short Stories for Strong Girls*, edited by Marilyn Singer (New York, NY: Scholastic Inc., 1998). / **12** Excerpt from 'The Day the Martian Landed" from *Farewell to the Twentieth Century: A Compendium of the Absurd* by Pierre Berton. © Pierre Berton. / **21** Excerpt from *The Random House Book of Jokes and Anecdotes: For Speakers, Managers, and Anyone Who Needs a Laugh* edited by Joseph Claro (New York, NY: Random House, Inc. / **23** Excerpt from "The Leaving" from *The Leaving* by Budge Wilson. © 1990 by Budge Wilson. Originally published by House of Anansi Press Limited. / **25** Excerpt from "Undersea Science" by Thomas Potts. © Thomas Potts. Originally published in *YES Mag* (Spring 1998). / **27** Excerpt from "Let's hear it (softly) for Rest Day" by Josie Marino and Jean-Francois Rioux from *The Globe and Mail* (February 22, 1999). / **30** Excerpt from "And the Lucky Winner Is . . ." by Monica Hughes from *On Spec*, Vol 2, No. 3 (Winter 1990). © 1990 The Copper Pig Writer's Society. / **36** "The Big Saw" from *More Poems For People* by Milton Acorn. Revised edition. (Toronto, ON: NC Press, 1972). / **50–51** Excerpt from "Monitoring Temperature Changes" by Dr. Otto B. Towes. / **54–55** Excerpt from "Based on the Novel" by Gordon Korman. © Gordon Korman Enterprises Inc., 20 Dersingham Crescent, Thornhill, ON, L3T 4E7. / **80** "The Red Wheelbarrow" by William Carlos Williams. © 1970 Florence Williams. / 159 Excerpt from "Character in Action: Ryan Schroer: Carrying the Torch" from *What Do You Stand For?: A Kid's Guide to Building Character* by Barbara A. Lewis, edited by Pamela Espeland (Minneapolis, MN: Free Spirit Publishing Inc.). / 159 Excerpt from "Horse Love" by Jane Smiley. / **160** Excerpt from *How We Make the TV Show: Behind the Scenes at Street Cents* by Barbara Kennedy, www.halifax.cbc.ca/strreetcents. / **160** Excerpt from "Capering" by Margaret Atwood.